The Emerging Worker

William A. Westley

and

Margaret W. Westley

The Emerging Worker

Equality and Conflict
in the
Mass Consumption Society

McGill–Queen's University Press
Montreal and London 1971

International Standard Book Number: 0 7735 0075 8
Library of Congress Catalog Card Number: 72 138976

*This book has been published with the help of
a grant from the Social Science Research Council of Canada,
using funds provided by the Canada Council.*

DESIGNED BY PETER MAHER

PRINTED IN CANADA

Contents

Tables

Introduction

The basic assumption of this book is that there have been for some time trends in the social, economic, psychological, and cultural experiences of workers in North America, and in other industrialized countries of Western Europe, which are producing a new kind of worker. This emerging worker, whose behaviour, like all other men's, is strongly influenced, if not determined, by his social environment, has a different view of himself and his relationship to his work and to society, and holds different ideas of what is a just distribution of profits and responsibility.

We should make it clear that we are not concerned with all workers or people who earn their living in these countries. Rather, we have chosen to concentrate on those workers who have been most affected in their work and social experience by the most modern technical, social, and economic developments of the mid-twentieth century: the semiskilled, highly paid, unionized worker and, to a lesser extent, the lower level white collar worker, whose experiences at work and in the society are becoming more and more like those of the semiskilled worker in the factory, and whose numbers are growing. To narrow the focus still more, it is the *young* worker, under thirty-five years, who is our prime subject, since he represents the first generation whose work experience has been under the main influences which we will discuss—high educational levels, high and rising incomes, high employment levels, and mass consumption

[1]

norms. He represents the "new" worker we see emerging, and we will attempt to explore and understand some of his attitudes and his relationships—primarily social relationships—to the major social institutions (that is, industrial management and unions) with which he is involved, and to the society at large.

It is essential to bear in mind that in this investigation of trends or experiences producing the new worker, we are not so much concerned with describing present-day society in North America and Western Europe as with concentrating on those elements which are emerging and which we believe will be of increasing importance during the coming decades. There are certainly differences in the economic, political, social, and cultural environments among the countries from which we have drawn illustrative material. We are aware of that. But we believe that certain experiences and values these countries have in common are more important, for our concerns, than their differences, and that technology and similar political and cultural values are propelling all the industrially developed Western countries in the same general direction, albeit with national variations. What we wish to emphasize is that we are attempting to isolate and identify common trends, particularly in Canada and the United States, and to a lesser extent in England and other Western European countries, and *not* to give exhaustive descriptions of the social environments of the countries from which our examples are drawn.

Since we are writing in Canada, a great deal of our material is drawn from Canadian experience, although the United States is almost equally important as a source of information and, being even more technologically advanced, is the epitome, in many ways, of the conditions which we wish to explore. Examples from British experience and occasionally from Western Europe are also included, although less often.

Affluence

There are several important conditions producing a new social environment in North American and Western European countries. These nations are affluent by comparison with the rest of the world; that is, the general level of real income in each country has reached a point where the majority of people have disposable income over and beyond their basic needs for food, clothing, and shelter. They have a highly developed technology, which continues to change and produce change at a geometric rate of progression. They have, to varying degrees, mass consumption economies, and increasingly, mass education systems, which, when wedded to democratic value systems, reinforce equalitarian tendencies. It goes without saying, also, that these countries are highly urbanized—a circumstance which many observers believe a necessary precondition to "takeoff" in economic development. Even Canada, the youngest and most recently urbanized of the group, was 50 per cent urban by 1941 and by 1961, the percentage was nearer to 70 per cent.[1]

The interest in underdeveloped, or developing nations, has, as a by-product, told us quite a bit about economically developed countries. It is doubtful that any proof is needed that the countries of North America and Western Europe are highly developed and wealthy by comparison with the rest of the world, but Kindleberger, among others, has established indices of development, which are, by inference, also indices of wealth. Examples of these indices are that the proportion of income spent for food is low; that a small proportion of the population is engaged in agriculture, while large proportions are engaged in manufacturing and service industries; that capital surplus exists for investment; that educational levels are high for most of the population; that urbanization is advanced and markets international; and that income distribution is tending toward equality.[2] These indices not only apply to the countries under consideration, but also were derived from the conditions found there.

Any discussion of affluent nations must take into account the fact that those nations, which have not yet managed to raise productivity enough to feed their populations dependably, fall relatively further behind as time passes. As Fourastié notes, "the two most numerous populations of the earth, the Chinese and the Indians, occupy a situation with respect to nutrition which is very similar to that of the French under Louis XIV"[3] and that "the world of today simultaneously contains communities that have hardly evolved at all in 2,000 years and others that are in full transition to a new human condition."[4]

The same can be said to some degree of each affluent nation: rising productivity and affluence does not affect everyone at the same time and in the same way. The spectacle of the United States engaging in an antipoverty program in the midst of the greatest, most widely dispersed wealth in the history of mankind is evidence of this. Canada also has her Indians and Eskimos, the inhabitants of the Maritimes and the Gaspé, and other pockets of people who have not shared equally in the general rise in the standard of living. There are considerable disparities between urban and rural income levels and between one region and another, and these regional differences have proved as difficult to eradicate as have the problems of the lowest income group, and more stubborn in Canada than in the United States. The Economic Council of Canada suggests that this may be because of poor utilization of human resources (too few people employed too irregularly) and low levels of productivity, neither of which has in the last forty years been much affected by rising prosperity and productivity elsewhere.[5] Nonunion labour has, also, not obtained a share of prosperity equal to that of organized labour. On the other hand, there is a tendency for wages to equalize in the long run, partly because the disparity leads either to unionization or, where possible, to labour mobility.

Besides these disadvantaged regions or groups, there are individuals whose deficiencies, psychological or physical, make them, at least under present methods of handling, perpetual wards of the society—the hard-core unemployables. There are also other kinds of unemployment or underemployment and poverty which are the result of technical change; the redundant or obsolete job or skill or product creates situations which leave some people stranded and unable to participate in the general well-being. In some cases, the technological difficulty may be compounded by social or psychological inability or unwillingness on the part of the individual to become mobile, to go where the opportunities are. These people are as surely bound to their soil or occupation as was the medieval peasant, and with very similar results.

In the United States, families still in the poverty category are those with heads sixty-five years of age and over, those with female heads, nonwhite families, and families with no one working at all.[6] In Canada, rural families should be added to this as a major category. For example, in 1961, 84 per cent of the farms in Newfoundland had a gross income of less than the $2,500 regarded as the poverty line for farm families. Showing regional disparities in Canada, N. K. Dhalla demonstrates that in 1961 in the Atlantic Provinces, 41.9 per cent of the prewar immigrants and native-born nonfarm families had an income of less than $3,000 (the general North American crude standard for measuring privation at the time). Montreal, on the other hand, had 3.6 per cent *less* than the national average of nonfarm families earning less than $3,000, and the south shore of the Gaspé had 26.8 per cent *more* than the national average, representing 26,342 families.[7]

But poverty is not new. It has been a formative influence in man's thinking since the beginning of recorded history. Ignorance and illiteracy are not new, nor is hopelessness. What is new is that a generation has grown up which, in the majority, in certain parts of the world has known in its working life only prosperity, full employment, and rising incomes, and has been the beneficiary of educational opportunities on an unprecedented scale. Average per capita incomes in current U.S. dollars rose in the United States from $2,115 in 1958 to $3,303 in 1967 and in Canada from $1,503 to $2,087 during the same period.[8] Put in a more impressive way, perhaps, median family income in the United States nearly tripled between 1947 and 1968.[9]

A nation begins to accumulate wealth when it no longer requires a major part of its labour force to provide the simple necessities of existence, that is, there will be enough food so that starvation no longer threatens important proportions of the population. Another way to say this is that the yearly increase in national product is regularly outstripping the yearly increase in population growth. This can only be accomplished through technical change which raises productivity, although a fall in the birthrate may help, too. "Enough to eat" is defined by generally accepted standards of the number of calories per day required to maintain normal functioning of the body, approximately twenty-seven hundred to twenty-eight hundred. Even today, only three-tenths of the human race, living in the Soviet Union, Western Europe, the United States, and the British Commonwealth have reached this level of living.[10]

The way in which this economic development occurs is of interest to us, since the forces set in motion lead, other things being equal, to a continually rising standard of living.

W. W. Rostow suggests that the development from subsistence to mass consumption societies can be divided into five stages: the traditional society; the preconditions for takeoff (in which time a nation begins to change in values, in scientific development, and in political and social institutions in such a way as to set the stage for industrialization); the takeoff (a stage reached when a nation begins rapid expansion of industries and application of technology to industry and to agriculture, when capital begins to accumulate, and strong political and social pressures for modernization develop); the drive to maturity (occurring when 10–20 per cent of the national income is regularly invested in the economy, permitting output regularly to outstrip the increase in population, and the economy has the technological and entrepreneurial skills to produce anything it wants to); and the mass consumption society (defined as a period when real income per head rises to a point where a large number of people can afford more than food, clothing, and shelter, and leading sectors of the economy shift toward production of durable consumers' goods and services).[11]

Rostow sets Canada's takeoff period as between 1896 and 1914, and that of the United States as between 1843 and 1860. Most of Western Europe had reached this stage by about 1870, except Great Britain whose takeoff period was much earlier, between 1783 and 1802.[12] He dates Canada's reaching technological maturity at about 1950, a stage reached by the United States by 1900, by Britain by 1850, and by Germany and France by 1910.[13]

Let us consider two of the salient characteristics that make the mass consumption economy different from the economy that preceded it. The first, as we have already mentioned, is that disposable income exists for a majority of the population. The second Rostow describes as:

> the structure of the working force changed in ways which increased not only the proportion of urban to total population, but also the proportion of the population working in offices or in skilled factory

jobs . . . aware of and anxious to acquire the consumption fruits of a mature economy. . . . It is in this post-maturity stage . . . that . . . Western societies have chosen to allocate increased resources to social welfare and security. The emergence of the welfare state is one manifestation of a society's moving beyond technical maturity; but it is also at this stage that resources tend increasingly to be directed to the production of consumers' durables and to the diffusion of services on a mass basis, if consumers' sovereignty reigns.[14]

Two important elements in the mass consumption society, then, are that a redistribution of income has occurred so that the group with middle-range incomes is larger than the groups at top and bottom, and that these middle-range incomes are high enough to afford some discretionary income. Dhalla shows that, in 1964, 60.1 per cent of Canadian households had incomes of more than $4,000 (using a household poverty base of $3,000), and he estimated that, by 1970, 82 per cent of households would have reached this level.[15] In the United States, in 1968, 77.6 per cent of families had incomes of $5,000 or more.[16]

An important factor supporting this income rise is the redistribution of the labour force from agriculture and other primary production to manufacturing (secondary) and service occupations (tertiary). Kindleberger shows, in charts based on United Nations statistics, that all the countries under consideration (North America and Western Europe) are high on income levels and low in proportions of the labour force engaged in agriculture, as compared to the rest of the world. The countries with the highest per capita income (United States, Canada, New Zealand, Australia, and Western Europe) also have the highest proportion of workers in secondary and tertiary production.[17]

2

Mass Consumption

If, then, North America and Western Europe have become "mass consumption societies," what is the meaning of this to the people who live there? It is a common myth and possibly a common occurrence that people accustomed to poverty do not know how to use material advantages even if they get them. There is a saying in certain regions of the United States that goes, "Give a West Virginian miner a bathroom and he'll keep coal in the bathtub." We suspect, however, that this kind of misuse occurs mostly when the material advantage, whether money or a bathroom, is a windfall, not to be relied on or not affecting in any basic way the standard of living of the recipient. To the West Virginian miner who has to contend with low wages, frequent layoffs, and a family ill-fed and ill-clothed, a bathtub seems irrelevant, if not outrageous. A place to keep fuel may be more important.

On the other hand, the experience of high wages and steady employment gives a man hope. He begins to think he can count on some security and even to improve his standard of living on a permanent basis. It then becomes worthwhile to work harder and to plan. What he usually prefers to buy are consumer durable goods, such as a house, a car, or a refrigerator, because these things represent a long-term improvement in his style of life.

The theories of J. M. Keynes in the late 1930s gave currency to the

idea that in production, full production, lay the solution to unemployment and many other socioeconomic ills. If production of goods keeps
the economy growing and prospering, these goods must, of course, find
a market, and a market that grows as productivity grows. At this point,
the behaviour of the consumer becomes economically important, as
important, George Katona argues, as capital behaviour. He points out
that consumers, in buying durable goods, are making an investment
and that their investments of this sort, by creating a demand, are contributing to the national income and to the enduring wealth of the
economy. His table 1, reproduced below, is an effort to compare U.S.
business expenditures with consumer expenditures, and he comments,
"Whatever the shortcomings of the statistical data, it is apparent that
consumers' investment expenditures on durable goods and housing are
at least as large as business investment expenditures."[1]

Katona proceeds to argue that, because consumers are less organized
and slower to respond as a group to economic fluctuations than is business, the effect of consumer investment in the economy is to smooth out
or reduce crises and fluctuations. It contributes, in other words, to
economic stability.

What the consumer wants to buy is a function of his perceived needs
and desires which are largely socially determined. The most important
determinant of *whether* and *when* a consumer will invest in durable
goods is his optimism or pessimism about the future, both his own and
that of the outside world.[2] Discretionary consumer demand is thus a
function both of ability and of willingness to buy, the latter made up of

TABLE 1

RECENT CHANGES IN WIDELY FLUCTUATING MONEY
OUTLAYS

(In Billions of Dollars)

ANNUAL OUTLAYS	1950	1955	1958	1960	1961	1962
Business construction and equipment	29.0	39.3	40.5	47.3	46.1	50.1
Consumer durable goods	30.4	39.6	37.6	44.8	43.7	47.5
Residential construction	14.1	18.7	18.0	21.1	21.0	23.3

NOTE: Reprinted by permission of the publisher from *The Mass Consumption
Society*, by George Katona (New York: McGraw Hill, 1964), table 1, p. 21.
Copyright 1964 by McGraw-Hill Inc.

motives, attitudes, and expectations which may change independently
of changes in income, although current income remains the most important determinant of *ability* to buy.

Not the only one, however. If the consumer's expectations of his
future income are optimistic, he may buy things he wants on an instalment plan, since his wife may go to work to help raise the general family
income or to make possible specific purchases, and he himself may take
on a second job. In this case, the consumer's *willingness* to buy changes
his *ability* to do so, and consumption is seen as no longer dependent on
income in the classical economic sense.

This is a very important development, if Katona is correct, and one
that concerns us here because it changes the relationship of the average
man to his economy and his society. He no longer feels helpless in the
face of economic forces over which he has no control and of which he
has little understanding. Business and government policies and activities
contribute enduring wealth, but so do those of the consumer, and consumers have a growing ability to determine the quantity, quality, and
timing of their contribution. The worker is free to decide how much
disposable or "discretionary" income he needs, how he will spend it, and
when. He begins to plan for the future.

The Role of Working Wives

Let us consider one fairly new source of increased income, the working
wife. Her role is of growing importance, since she works not only to
help provide the subsistance needs of the family, but often to improve
the standard of living or to meet instalment payments.

In the last twenty-five years, particularly since 1941, there has been
an increase in labour force participation rates of married women over
the age of thirty-five and of middle-class status. At the same time, there
has been a decisive change in the age pattern or "participation profile,"
in which young married women drop out of the labour force during
child-bearing years, and then return. In the United States, the proportion of wives working doubled between 1940 and 1960. Since they are
more likely to be employed when they are between the ages of thirty-
five and fifty-four, it is clear that their earnings are influential in helping
family income reach its peak at this time. The difference between male
income and total family income is smallest when the husband is between

twenty-five and thirty-four, a time when the smallest proportions of wives are working.[3]

Of far greater importance than age in determining the labour force participation of married women is education. For women as a whole, regardless of marital status, the higher the level of education, the higher the level of labour force participation at each age, no matter what income her husband makes.[4] One of the tentative explanations offered for this correlation is that education may increase a woman's tastes for a higher standard of material living for herself and her family, and that this would act as a stimulus to her going to work.[5]

However, while the trend for middle-class women to work is clear, and while it is often fairly affluent families who supplement their income, present statistics do indicate that within any occupational category the wives of husbands earning less than others in each category are more likely to be employed. Hence, although labour force projections may point to a gradual upsurge in employed women from middle and upper socioeconomic brackets, in general, the lower the husband's income, the more likely his wife is to work.[6]

In sum, the basic transition in the past twenty years has been away from the situation in which women were forced into employment, with their labour the primary source of family income, to one in which women were drawn into employment to raise family living standards and for other related reasons. Clearly, the capacity and willingness of wives to get jobs has added to the family's capacity to acquire "discretionary income."

The Use of Consumer Credit

Another major new factor contributing to increased income is the astounding growth of the use of credit, particularly by those groups in the lower half of the income scale. The Porter Commission on Banking and Finance in Canada reported that, following 1945, rising levels of income and employment, low levels of personal debt, the rising output of durable goods to replace and extend the aging stock of such assets in the hands of consumers, and other factors affecting the willingness and ability of individuals to incur debt, led to a strong consumer credit demand and the rapid growth of institutions prepared to meet it.[7] Total consumer credit jumped from $835 million in 1948 to $2,517 million ten years later, and continued to grow rapidly through succeeding years, reaching the $7,076 million mark in 1965. The most rapid increase has been in instalment credit for durable goods. While it is true that a continuous rise in national income has paralleled the rapid growth of aggregate consumer credit, the ratio of consumer credit to personal disposable income has also risen steadily. Canadian consumer credit of all kinds now amounts to about 20.2 per cent of personal income, as compared to 7.5 per cent in 1948.

It should be made clear, however, that although consumer credit has increased in size relative to income since 1948, aggregate consumer debt has risen much less than aggregate consumer assets; the Porter Commission claims that the average household in Canada reports total debt equivalent to only 18 per cent of assets, with three-quarters of this total indebtedness in the form of mortgages and not instalment debt. In the United States, figures are similar. The survey also revealed that 50 per cent of the households in their study of consumer finances had no instalment or mortgage debt, a further 29 per cent had repayment commitments equal to between 30 per cent and 49 per cent of income. (For description of sample of consumer finances, see bibliography, George Katona et al.) Although some consumers may incur instalment debt beyond their capacity to handle, this does not seem to be the case in general.

The Porter Commission discovered that those in Canada who used credit the most were lower income groups, followed by average and then high income groups, although charge accounts were most frequent at the higher income levels. In the United States, however, the highest proportion of spending units owing instalment debt had incomes between five thousand dollars and ten thousand dollars.[8] Families who expect their income to rise use credit more than those who expect it to stay the same or decline. Young people, possibly because they are in a stage of life when incomes normally do rise, use credit far more than older age groups; in fact, there is a gradual decline with age. The Porter Commission also found that labourers, skilled and unskilled, use credit more than any other occupational group, followed by clerical workers. Farmers and retired workers use it least. Finally, steady employment causes people to buy on the instalment plan, whereas unemployment, periodic or chronic, discourages the use of credit.[9]

Consumer credit, then, is used primarily by young people who are steadily employed at semiskilled or unskilled labour (followed in frequency of use by skilled, clerical, and other middle income occupations) and whose incomes are rising.

Thus the high wages and increasing job opportunities resulting from advancing technology have provided the majority of North American families with enough "discretionary income" to enable them to gain more material advantages offered by their societies. Working wives and consumer credit make it possible for the lower and middle income family to stabilize their standard of living or to improve it, at the discretion of the members, and help shorten the gap of advantage between one social and economic group and another.

Given the ability of the consumer to buy, what does he buy? Do consumption patterns change with the arrival of the mass consumption society?

Consumption Patterns

Leaving aside for the moment the question of whether a house purchase has the same meaning for a working man as for a middle-class entrepreneur, there is considerable evidence that there is a tendency for everyone to want the same things and even to buy the same things. The difference between a car bought by a man making six thousand dollars a year and one bought by a man making ten thousand dollars is in the price or quality, but both will have cars. Patterns of family expenditures in Canada for 1964 by age, income, occupation, and education of the head of the family show a surprising consistency in the proportions of income spent for various goods and services.[10] Within occupational categories, managers spend exactly the same proportion of their income on household appliances as do labourers. Their expenditure on car purchase amounted to 6.1 per cent of their income, whereas skilled craftsmen spent 6.2 per cent. Although absolute amounts increase with income, the proportions do not vary much, suggesting that it is quantity and quality of goods rather than the nature of the expenditure that changes with increased income. The only really striking difference in expenditure patterns is related to education. The higher the education of the head of a household, the more money is spent on education by the family, and this difference moves (except for a slight dip in the "partial secondary school" category) in a steady curve from .6 per cent of the income of a person with primary school education to 2 per cent of the income of a university graduate.

One interesting point to be observed is that, with income held constant, the family of a twenty-five-year-old spends approximately the same amount as that of a forty-five-year-old. For example, the average expenditure for all income groups of age twenty-five to thirty-four in 1964 was $6,566, and the average expenditure for those of age forty-five to fifty-four was $6,734. This statistic suggests that there is a standard expenditure package which a family takes on almost as soon as it is formed and which varies little with age. This trend indicates a very important change in social patterns that may be traced directly to affluence, but also, as we shall see, to education and other experiences in the mass consumption society. In the past, there was an age-grading system which dictated that young people had to save and earn the fruits of comfort and security over a lifetime. They expected and were expected to have life a little harder at the beginning, with fewer of the material things of life than their parents had. However, as the parent of any teen-ager knows, young people now expect to have whatever their parents' style of life affords them. Besides, their parents have trained them, as has the society at large, that there is no particular virtue in either saving or waiting for what they want. They want immediately what everyone else of their income, occupational, and educational level has.

Insofar as we can tell, people in the forty-five to fifty-four age group have changed their pattern of consumption during their lifetime. The man who was fifty-one in 1964 was twenty-four in 1937. We can therefore compare the expenditures of a family of a twenty-five-year-old in 1937 with a similar family of today. The Dominion Bureau of Statistics figures were, in 1937–38, divided into French and British families, and we must further allow for the change in dollar value of different goods and services. Nevertheless, the pattern of expenditures at that time is quite different from those shown in the 1964 DBS tables.[11] In 1964, for example, for families in all income groups whose head was between twenty-five and thirty-four, food represented 20.1 per cent of the family budget, shelter 17.4 per cent, clothing 7.8 per cent, household operation 4.6 per cent, and transportation 12.7 per cent, to list a few of the biggest changes. The proportions spent on the first four items have diminished since 1937, while that spent on transportation (including purchase and operation of a car) has doubled.

These statistics suggest that the man who grew up in the preaffluent, depression-ridden thirties now has acquired the same tastes, the same view of the "good things of life" as his son who has never known anything but affluence. The difference in experience and values which these two periods are felt to represent apparently has little effect on consumption patterns. It seems evident that consumption patterns in a mass consumption society tend toward uniformity for all age, income, and occupational groups.

Leisure Consumption

Another important indication of the existence of what David Reisman and Howard Roseborough have called "the standard package"[12] is in the use of leisure. The increased leisure on a mass basis is one of the characteristics of an affluent society, and leisure expenditures support many service, recreational, and even some basic industries, such as the automobile industry.

There is evidence to suggest that the availability of leisure time, in combination with discretionary income, may offer a way out of the rigidity of status definitions based on one's occupation or work hierarchies. For example: "As a man from Mars would see it, they (the $4,000 a year family and the $20,000 a year family) live equally good lives because they both have cars and plenty of food. It is doubtful that he would see any important differences between the public course golfers and the White Sulphur Springs variety."[13] In other words, on his own time a man can and does pursue the same activities and often in very much the same way as his boss. Both will have and use TV sets, automobiles, fishing rods, do-it-yourself kits; both may own or rent summer cottages and go skiing in the winter. We do not mean to imply that the amount of time or money, or even the proportion of income spent on these things, will be the same for the worker as for the boss, but simply to indicate that here again they want and, by and large, have the same things.

Denney observes with regard to American expenditures on leisure that, "It is the similarity, not the difference, that is most striking in these patterns. The steady increase in all expenditures as American families go up the income ladder had the odd side effect that they all buy the same package of life and leisure, wrapped up in a different style."[14] Our statistics on Canadian family expenditures indicate that the same can be said of Canada.

More evidence supporting the theory that leisure pursuits are an important new way of obtaining status and prestige and of breaking out of class hierarchies is demonstrated by statements comparing work and leisure made by British workers to Ferdynand Zweig. One, for example, said, "I am working class only in the works but outside I am like anyone else." And another, "Here I am a worker but outside I am a human being."[15] As Reisman comments, with regard to lower income groups in the United States, "These people look to their leisure time and con-sumership for the satisfactions and pride previously denied them by the social order."[16]

The student of industrial relations, however, should note that, in general, higher income rather than more leisure is preferred by all workers, regardless of age or occupation, at least up to the higher brackets of income. The Survey Research Center in 1960 found that in a national U.S. sample 48 per cent of men and 51 per cent of women felt they had about the right amount of leisure; 37 per cent of men and 36 per cent of women felt they had too little. Those who said they had too much leisure are predominantly older people.[17] Apparently, the group that feels it has too little leisure are those under forty-five who have an income of more than seventy-five hundred dollars. Whether this is be-cause they are in the hard-working years of their career or job, or because income is reaching a point where "discretionary time" becomes more interesting than "discretionary income" is not clear. Zweig found that British workers prefer to work overtime, when possible, rather than to take extra leisure, because they regard the extra money as more im-portant.[18] An article in *Fortune* magazine on early retirement plans for workers in the United States indicated that older people do not want to retire early and often do so only to take other work.[19] More evidence showing that income is considered more important than leisure was found by Hecksher and de Grazia in the *Harvard Business Review* study of executive leisure. When asked whether they would prefer more leisure or increased income, 71.8 per cent of executives under forty years of age said they would prefer more income. Of those over fifty years, 55.1 per cent would prefer more leisure, but this group is more likely to have reached an income peak already, and one which satisfied most of their desires. For the entire group sampled, 54.7 per cent would choose higher income.[20] This demonstrates the primacy of rising income and suggests that union demands for a shorter work week and early retirement do not reflect workers' desire for more leisure time, but are efforts to spread the work and avoid layoffs.

The Importance of Consuming

The standard package of consumption changes continually as to specific commodities, as new ones appear on the market and old ones become obsolete, and as the content of the "good life" is redefined. Although some observers worry about what will happen when everyone in the society has all the goods they can possibly use, others maintain that while desire for a particular object, for instance a house or a car, may be satiated, the satisfaction of this want gives rise to others, such as house furnishings, and that therefore there is no end to the desire to buy. In any case, it is clear that what is enough for this year is, for most people, not quite enough for next year and that there is a continual satiation of changing needs. That this factor contributes substantially to our technical progress and prosperity is shown by D. Pécaut in a report to the Organization for Economic Cooperation and Development on workers' attitudes to technical change. He hypothesizes, on the basis of studies of European and American workers, that the greater the extent of a worker's dedication to and participation in these continuously changing consumption patterns or "norms," the more he is willing to accept change in his work, and to move geographically or occupationally to take advantage of opportunity—which, of course, brings higher incomes.[21] Technical progress and prosperity depend upon a working force of people who can adapt to change in these ways.

We have shown that mass consumption societies have an economy geared to the production and consumption of consumer goods and services, and that the role of the consumer as investor and contributor of wealth is now as important as that of government or business in the continued growth and stability of the economy. If continued high level consumption and production depend, at least partly, on consumer willingness and ability to buy, then the consumer's optimistic faith in the economy and in his own future become important considerations of public policy. Whether the desire to buy a product is derived from advertising, from the mass media, from the opinion leaders, or from a man's co-workers and neighbours, or from a combination of these, the fact seems to be that in having enough discretionary income to participate in the "good life" as defined by his society, a majority of citizens have, at the same time, found an escape from demeaning or frustrating work and from social stratification which defines some people as less worthy than others because of the work they do, or the conditions under which they live. These form powerful motives, evidently, to increase income, by whatever means possible, and even, if the future looks rosy, to barter some future gains for immediate ones. The carrot of increasing affluence produces better results than the stick of economic insecurity, as Galbraith, among others, has noted.[22]

It may be important at this point to call attention to what we believe

is a basic change in motivation for consumption. Kindleberger points
out that:

> Today the world over, however, people have become much more
> responsive to their peers, aware of the efficacy of the public relations
> man and advertising, and in consequence readier to suppress and
> alter the characteristics acquired in their childhood. Fashions extend
> to child rearing, changes in which rupture the continuity of national
> character. Consumption changes from conspicuous to self-conscious.
> The demonstration effect leads people to strive to forsake their tra-
> ditions in favor of the consumption standard of others, studied
> through international communication by press, radio, magazines,
> books, motion pictures . . . the desire to conform in consumption
> standards may be so strong that, given the minimum of resources and
> capital, impediments in the national culture will be overcome.[23]

Kindleberger was speaking of nations, but the same can be said of individuals. A man who sees a new gadget advertised on TV, or the girl
who tries X shampoo because of a magazine advertisement is not necessarily "keeping up with the Joneses." They are more likely to buy the
product because they believe it will benefit them, or because it is associated in their minds with the "good life." We would not maintain that
conspicuous consumption, or the desire to put one's friends down, has
disappeared from the repertoire of human motives, but we would suggest
that it is not enough to explain the phenomenon called "mass consumption," and, in fact, that it is not even the most important motive. Mass
consumption has become the way to the good life and the means of
supporting the high production economy. Whether it can or will continue
to have this semisacred quality is a question we will consider later.

3

The Importance
of Education

Rising Levels of Education

One of the most significant changes associated with affluence and the technologically advanced society is that the level of education for the whole population rises. To take only a few examples from the Western nations, in Sweden between 1866 and 1939 the size of the school population increased by a ratio of 1 to 1.4, while the number receiving the baccalaureate (a degree attained at about age twenty there) had jumped in the ratio of 1 to 9 in the same period. France, which was rather slower to develop in this and in certain other aspects of technological maturity, has nonetheless increased its number of young people in postprimary education from a proportion of around twelve per thousand in 1880 to a proportion of fifty per thousand of the population under twenty-one years of age.[1] In Canada, the proportion of the population from five to twenty-four years of age atttending school has moved from 49.3 per cent in 1921 to 65.7 per cent in 1961.[2] Looking at it another way, in Canada, in 1965, 24.1 per cent of the population aged twenty to twenty-four had finished high school, whereas of those people sixty-five years and over (who would have attended high school around 1915), only 12 per cent finished high school. The figures for the United States during this same fifty-year period show an even more remarkable rise in the proportion completing high school—from 14.8 per cent to 44.3 per cent.[3]

At the university level in Canada in 1966–67, 13.4 per cent out of 100 people in the eighteen to twenty-four year age group were in college, as compared to 4 per cent out of 100 twenty years ago. In the United States, about 20 per cent out of 100 in this age group were in college during that year, and it has been estimated that by 1970–71 we will have reached a level in Canada of about 18.3 per cent attendance compared to 21 per cent in the United States.[4] The United States leads the world in the proportion of its population enrolled in schools, of course, as it does in per capita national income, in productivity, and in other indices of wealth. A recent publication comparing developments in secondary education among countries affiliated with the Office of Economic Co-operation and Development shows that the United States had over 80 per cent of its population aged fourteen to eighteen in secondary schools, as of 1964. Other studies using similar dates and age groupings show Canada and the Netherlands to have 60–80 per cent enrolment, and France and Germany to have one of 40–60 per cent. Italy, England, and Wales have only 20–40 per cent of the appropriate age group in school. Spain and Portugal have a lower percentage.[5]

There may be many national and cultural differences accounting for the educational gap between countries, one of the most important of which is a heritage of an élitist tradition, in which a ruling class needed training and presumably few others did. The United States had less of this tradition than the European countries. Such traditions are disappearing slowly, as evidenced by the fact that France has already raised the compulsory school attendance age to sixteen years, and England will do so in 1971.

However, there is another factor which may be involved as well. A common "takeoff" problem that has plagued economic planners around the world is that the national wealth and productivity which depend on an educated work force are also the means of providing the capital and the human investment necessary for a mass education system. The richer the nation, the more money it has to pour into education, and the better it can afford to keep its young people in school for the necessary extra years.

Presumably the United States will soon reach a saturation point, at least with regard to secondary school attendance, and then the other industrial countries will begin to close the gap. As Illing and Zsigmond in a recent study for the Economic Council of Canada remark: "The projections imply a school enrolment ratio of 91 per cent of those in the 14–17 age group by the mid-1970's . . . the enrolment rates of this group in Canada reached about the same level in the mid-1960's as had existed in the U.S. in the early 1950's (around 78 per cent). By the mid-1970's, the ratio in Canada is expected to reach a level about equivalent to the present U.S. ratio, implying a substantial further narrowing of the enrolment ratio gap between the two countries over the coming decade."[6]

Fourastié has spelled out the significance of the educational advance. "The increase in the school population appears . . . not as the result of fashion or of transitory impulses, but as a structural phenomenon related to the whole of contemporary economic evolution. This increase results directly from the rise in the average level of living and from the reduction of the duration of work necessary for a given national production. It is thus a direct consequence of technical progress, and will continue as long."[7]

This experience of more years of education, we believe, changes workers' attitudes in some ways that are crucial. For one thing, it leads them to believe that they have a *right* to some of the improvements in their way of life which affluence leads them to hope and plan for.

Demand for Higher Education

As we show in chapter 1, the emergence of an affluent nation presupposes the existence of a level of scientific and technical training among the population to begin, to carry through, and to sustain changes in the methods of production such that the economy can produce more than its inhabitants need for survival. Education, then, is necessary, at least for a minority, to start the process of economic development. As technology advances, it requires more people who are sufficiently educated to take on work that becomes increasingly mental rather than physical. That this process is actually occurring is easily demonstrated. In Canada, according to Noah Meltz, the median years of schooling for males in each occupation for all occupations has risen from 7.5 years in 1941 to 9 years in 1961. Managers at that time had a median of 10.6 years of education as compared to 9.1 in 1941; labourers and agriculture workers have come from 6.7 and 6.6 years respectively to 7.2 years of schooling; and service workers from 7.5 years in 1941 to 8.2 in 1961.[8]

The Department of Labour's study, *Acquisition of Skills*, found that among skilled tradesmen, after 1945, the rate of completion of and/or attendance at secondary school rose noticeably. For example:

Electronic technicians: From 50 per cent completing during the war years to 74 per cent completing in the post-1945 period.
Senior draughtsmen: 69 per cent completing secondary school after

1945, said to be "considerably higher" than in the earlier periods.

Tool and die makers: Completion rate was lower after 1945 than during the war, but attendance at secondary school increased from 67 per cent in the pre-1930 period to 88 per cent after 1945.

Sheet metal workers: Attendance was highest in the post-1945 period, when it was 65 per cent, compared with 29 per cent in the pre-1930 period.[9]

This study then goes on to explain that educational requirements for all these trades have risen at least as rapidly as has the level of education.

A major reason for the higher level of education among the formally trained is that, so far as organized training in industry, such as apprenticeship, is concerned, a certain level of educational attainment has usually been required, though this may vary from trade to trade. Thus education has been used in the past, and is being used to an even greater degree in the present, as a screening device for the selection of workers for formal training programs in industry. This situation has usually not prevailed in the case of workers trained through informal means. The resulting disparity between the education of formally and informally trained workers may be even greater today because of the *trend in industry towards raising still further the academic entrance requirements* for in-plant training programs for the development of skilled workers and technicians. This trend is a reflection of a technology, increasing in complexity, which dictates the need for workers with a better knowledge of mathematics and science and a better educational background generally. It is only to be expected that, in these circumstances, the selection of candidates for in-plant training programs will favour those with a higher level of education.[10]

Meltz found that, between 1951 and 1961, demand for persons with thirteen-plus education, that is, post high school, increased even more than the supply and that the demand came not only from the professions, but to a greater extent, from managerial and clerical occupations. In fact, every nonprofessional occupation experienced an upsurge in its thirteen-plus proportion. He continues: "Thus, although the increase in the level of education of persons in the labour force shifted the supply curve to professional occupations, the demand for professionals and the demand for non-professionals with higher levels of education appears to have risen even faster."[11]

It is interesting that Meltz found this demand outrunning supply only after 1951. There had been little change in the level of education in nonprofessional occupations before that time. This coincides with Rostow's date for Canada's entering the stage of high mass consumption, when affluence may be said to have become really widespread.

We can assume then that technologically advanced countries have and will continue to have rapidly rising levels of education for the majority of their citizens. Accompanying this are increasingly high academic requirements for jobs at all levels of the economy. This is the result both of the greater supply of educated people available and of the greater intellectual demands made by modern technology.

Education and National Economic Growth

A number of economists have, in the last few years, been trying to find ways to estimate the contribution of education to the economic growth of a nation. The assumption is that education is an investment in human capital, which in turn contributes some definable economic value, that is, wealth and progress, to the economic system, much as physical capital does when put to use. The methods of measuring this elusive factor have been difficult to achieve and probably are still crude. However, Edward Denison has estimated that increased education contributed 23 per cent of the growth in the U.S. national income between 1929 and 1957, as compared with 15 per cent contributed by capital inputs during this period.[12]

Bertram has estimated that in Canada between the years 1911 and 1961 the rise in the educational level has accounted for almost one-fourth of the rise in the productivity per employed person. He further estimates that improved education accounted for 12 per cent of the growth in national income between 1911 and 1961.[13]

One of the interesting uses to which this measuring of the economic value of education has been put is in estimating the optimum level of educational investment for underdeveloped countries. Nalla Gouden, for example, shows that for India the highest rate of return on educational investment in 1967 would be in a school system designed to permit every Indian child to complete primary school, whereas at India's stage of development, investment in secondary and university systems would be a poor one.[14] Studies by the Department of Labour as well as Meltz's statistics demonstrate that Canada needs the general educational level of the population to be raised. One report on manpower in Canada points out that, "if demand is to be met, training and educational facilities at all levels of the educational system from primary school to postgraduate courses will have to be expanded in an orderly fashion."[15] The report states that the most pressing needs are at the level of university and postsecondary technical training. Canada has evidently done well so far as primary education is concerned, but has failed to invest adequately in providing secondary and particularly university education. This is borne out by the fact that until now Canada has had to depend on immigration for a large proportion of its professional and skilled manpower.[16]

Education and Individual Income

Education adds not only to the wealth of a nation, but also to the wealth of the individual. In fact, this relationship is as nearly a perfect correlation as we can expect in any study of human experience. Bertram has shown clearly that throughout a man's life his level of education determines his income and that a university degree makes the most significant difference to this income. A man with a university degree can expect that his earnings will rise from $7,000 at the beginning of his career to around $11,000 by the end of his career, whereas the man who attends university but does not finish will, on the average, only progress from $5,000 to $6,500. Every other level of education commands a proportionally lower salary with less expectation of improvement.[17] Miller has shown that in the United States not only is the income gradient steadily upward from $2,551 for a person with less than eight years of education in 1958 to $9,206 for a college graduate, but that since 1939 the salary difference between the lowest and the highest levels has widened. Whereas in 1939 the person with an elementary education earned about 39 per cent of the college graduate's income, in 1958 his income was 33 per cent of the salary which the college graduate could expect to receive. Thus, the gap has widened by about 6 per cent.[18]

Lest one assume that these differences are due to the selective process whereby those of favoured cultural or socioeconomic backgrounds and of high intelligence are the ones that continue in the educational system, this theory has been disproved by a study made in the United States by Wolfle-Smith of a sample of nearly three thousand men graduated from Illinois, Minnesota, and Rochester high schools.[19] They were studied about seventeen years after graduation. The results show that with intelligence held constant, graduates in the lowest 45 per cent of I.Q. test scores with a college degree made the same income as did people with a higher I.Q. but who had less education; they made considerably more than those with the highest I.Q. but who had only a high school education. Another equally interesting finding, shown by the Wolfle-Smith survey, is that the income of a labourer's son, if he gets a college education, exceeds that of the son of a professional man or manager who fails to get a college degree. The worker's son who finishes college may make, on the average, one thousand dollars more than the professional's son, if the latter had *some* college education, and thirteen hundred dollars more if the professional's son only finished high school. (See table 2.)

As S. M. Miller remarks: "The general rise in the level of education has not reduced the importance of education; it has shifted upward the

TABLE 2

MEDIAN SALARIES OF ILLINOIS AND ROCHESTER MEN WITH DIFFERENT POST–HIGH SCHOOL EDUCATION BY OCCUPATION OF FATHER

FATHER'S OCCUPATION	EDUCATION AFTER HIGH SCHOOL GRADUATION*		
	None or Technical School	Some College	One College Degree or More
Professional and semiprofessional	$5,200 (12)	$5,500 (24)	$7,600 (141)
Owners and managers	5,000 (58)	5,800 (43)	7,400 (145)
Sales and clerical	5,183 (54)	5,200 (38)	7,300 (92)
Service	4,611 (19)	6,200 (9)	7,200 (24)
Labour	4,863 (208)	5,700 (98)	6,500 (161)
Farm	4,176 (59)	5,400 (21)	6,000 (37)

SOURCE: E. F. Denison, "Proportion of Income Differentials among Education Groups due to Additional Education: The Evidence of the Wolfle-Smith Survey," in *The Residual Factor and Economic Growth*, OECD, Paris, 1964, p. 94, table A 6. The study, "The Occupational Value of Education for Superior High School Graduates," appeared in the *Journal of Higher Education* 27, no. 4 (April, Graduates," appeared in the *Journal of Higher Education* 27, no 4 (April, 1956): 206.

*Figures in parentheses refer to number of cases dealt with.

breaking point where education leads to high or low income. It is certainly better to be a high school graduate than a dropout, but it is much better to be a college graduate."[20]

Education and Mobility

Bertram points out several ways in which a higher level of education improves not only the income of the worker, but also his opportunity and capacity to be mobile, to adapt to technological change, and to improve his occupational status. "Further years of schooling provide what has been termed a 'financial option' return, or the value of the opportunity to obtain still further education. Two other benefits that appear to be important are non-monetary 'opportunity options' involving wider individual employment choices, which education permits, and opportunities for 'hedging' against the vicissitudes of technological change."[21]

This capacity to be mobile, to take advantage of opportunities is, as we have shown, essential to both the individual and national prosperity. As Peitchinis says, "Economic expansion cannot be attained and sustained without labour mobility."[22]

Richard Centers has shown that educational levels are positively related to occupational mobility, that is, to moving up in job status, which, in turn, becomes a kind of social mobility, particularly for those sons whose fathers were in the lower status occupations. For example, of those manual workers' sons who had a better education than their fathers, 53 per cent also had a higher occupational status.[23] Palmer came to the same conclusion in her study of labour mobility in six major American cities. She found that education above certain limits provides roughly equal access to the white collar occupations for sons of fathers from all occupational groups, while the lack of it severely limits access, and that "thus the educational opportunities available to sons of fathers at different levels of skill are the primary influence in determining the levels attained by the sons."[24]

Another way to estimate the mobility value of education is by observing the levels of education usually found at different occupational levels. Lipset and Bendix have included a table in their study of social mobility which shows clearly that the higher the status, the higher the educational level of the occupation. Managers, officials, and proprietors seem to show a slight deviation from this pattern, but it should be remembered that this category includes owners of small businesses. They are often immigrants of little education, manual workers trying to break out of factory work, or people with no particular training, all of whom bring the educational level of the category down below what one might expect. In the United States in 1950, 85.6 per cent of professional and technical people had at least a high school education compared to 56.4 per cent of clerical workers and 11.6 per cent of labourers.[25]

In discussing the rising educational *requirements* for different occupations, we have already quoted Meltz's statistics (see p. 23) showing that over time the educational levels in each occupational category are rising in Canada. The same study also serves to show that higher education permits eligibility for higher status occupations.

So far as geographical mobility is concerned, it can be inferred that education opens the mind to possibilities for advancement and wider experience, and as our political attitudes survey will show, it certainly adds to the sense of potency, of capacity to control and manipulate the environment, and reduces fears based on inability to understand the changing environment. All these things, one can assume, make it easier for a man to leave the safety of the familiar community to take advantage of some opportunity beckoning elsewhere. However, we have been unable to find definite proof of this, partly because, although the highly educated may be willing to move, they often do not find it necessary. The unskilled and the semiskilled, who have in general a low educational level, actually hold more different jobs, as Reynolds discovered, but not always as a matter of choice, nor even because of a desire to achieve a better position.[26]

That education, especially general academic education, is an aid to technical mobility is made clear by the examples showing that factory training programs usually are made available to those having higher educational qualifications (see Department of Labour study, pp. 23–24). Not only is learning new methods probably easier for those with better backgrounds in mathematics and science, but they are given opportunities to become "technically mobile" over workers with less education. A study of automated steel plants in six European countries found that in the two countries, France and Holland, where there were differences in educational attainment among the workers, the workers with higher general education were promoted over older, more experienced workers when automation occurred. Furthermore, younger men, with more educational qualifications, were more likely to be earning higher wages after the change to automated production. This was not true where seniority determined promotion changes, of course, but where it did occur, it seemed to be largely a reflection of the greater ability of the more educated to adapt to new technical requirements.[27]

This ability to take advantage of what Bertram has called the "financial option" return of education is also demonstrated by participation rates in adult education. These results are comparable to the findings concerning the greater opportunities workers with high general educational levels have to participate in factory training programs. However, they apply to the whole population. Venn's study of retraining programs in the United States shows that for both blue and white collar workers, previous educational attainment was the biggest single factor influencing participation in adult education programs. By comparison, the influence of occupation and income is not very important.[28]

Lipset and Bendix believe that "education . . . has become the principal avenue for upward mobility in most industrialized nations,"[29] and that this is an important fact underlying the confidence of the American worker that he can improve his position in life, either in status or in income or both, if he had a "good" education. And our review of the literature on this subject shows that this is, in fact, statistically a realistic assumption. That this idea is firmly planted, especially in the minds of workers in the blue collar occupations, has been demonstrated by many researchers as we shall see in the chapter on life styles. Purcell, for example, found that packinghouse workers wanted their children to get an education so they would not have to be packinghouse workers.[30] Chinoy found that auto workers who had ceased to hope for themselves transferred their aspirations to their children and believed education would give them a better life.[31] Berger, studying auto workers in a new California suburb, found that an "overwhelming majority of the sample say they want college education for their sons."[32]

In view of these responses, there is a poignancy in the findings of Fortin and Tremblay that of 362 family heads in and around Ste. Julienne, Quebec, 59 per cent advised their young people to work for wages, preferably in the city (51 per cent), rather than to become farmers.[33] In another study of three metal-working plants in Montreal, Dofny and David found that when rural workers come to the city to work for wages, they are content for quite awhile because they expect to realize their dreams, whereas those whose fathers were wage earners before them had given up all but the smallest aspirations for themselves. However, 80 per cent believe that through education their children can substantially improve their position in life.[34] This same belief in the power of education to provide children with the opportunities the parents have not had is an important factor in the current exodus of Newfoundland families from the outports to the cities and towns. The parents are no longer willing to allow their children to grow up illiterate.[35]

Education and Consumption Norms

Education apparently has little effect on consumption patterns except in a few things. More money will be spent on education, and the higher the educational level, the more money will be spent on books, magazines, and newspapers.[36] An American study shows that there are no differences in leisure activities, other than reading.[37] There may be some difference in the quality of goods bought as education increases, but Canadian expenditure patterns by education of head do not show, as we said before, any significant difference in *what* is bought, except in expenditures on education.

The most important effect of education on consumption is that it produces confidence in the worker and the expectation of continued progress; these factors, in turn, increase his willingness to buy. Alex Inkeles, for example, quotes two international studies of the relationship between education and optimism about the future to show that "those who are better educated and trained, and hold more responsible positions, will be more optimistic specifically about those situations where the possibility of man's mastery of himself or his environment is involved."[38] Dofny and David found that among Montreal workers (English-speaking, French-speaking, old and new Canadians), the higher the educational level, the more optimistic they were about the possibility of improving their personal position in the plant and the working man's position in the society at large.[39]

Education, because of its association with increased income and occupational mobility, also produces the means to buy. Finally, this combination of rising income and education produces an equalitarianism in the family and in the society which results in more women getting higher education and joining the labour force. The higher the educational level of wives, the more likely they are to work, and this factor is almost as important as the income of the husband in determining whether or not they do work outside the home. They do not work entirely for economic reasons, but their jobs do add to the family purchasing power.

Rising Expectations
and Dissatisfaction

Our investigation of the effects of rising levels of education leads us to assume that an individual will feel that an increase in his education will produce a corresponding increase in his status and income. This attitude prevails even when education is compulsory. Compulsory education might, in fact, be regarded as a way of raising the expectations of a society artificially, or even against the will of some members. In Nigeria, for example, when compulsory school education was introduced, all the graduates refused to work because they knew that educated men stayed in offices and, by their definition, did not work. Therefore, unless levels of productivity and wealth of an economy can continue to provide opportunities for either status or income improvement, a great deal of dissatisfaction may be expected among workers whose jobs offer less than they feel their education entitles them to receive.

There is some evidence that this attitude already occurs, at all levels of the occupational structure, whenever the person feels that, by virtue of his education, he has a right to a higher position than the one he occupies. Drucker castigates American management for "the tendency to make the jobs of the young, educated people as unimportant as possible, as undemanding as possible and as boring as possible."[40] He believes this to be a major reason for business failing to attract and keep the brightest and best-trained young men. In a study of engineers and scientists, 61 per cent of whom were under thirty-five and 58 per cent of whom had college degrees, Danielson found dissatisfaction was common, and resulted from what these professionals felt to be inadequate wages, not enough interesting work, and promotions which came too slowly. As one supervisor admitted: "They are not promoted and paid according to their abilities. I think their big problem is that they feel their advancement will be slow. . . . Some of this comes from the fact that they get the impression in school that they're going to shoot ahead fast . . . I think they get told by somebody in school that they should demand so much and nothing less."[41]

Finally, Kornhauser, in a study of the mental health of U.S. workers, found that among unskilled and semiskilled workers self-esteem and satisfaction with life decreased as educational levels rose, but that personal morale and sociability increased. "Personal morale" was defined as a tendency toward social trust or distrust, a generalized pessimism or optimism about life. "Sociability" refers to one's attitudes toward other people, described on a continuum from gregariousness to social withdrawal. Kornhauser interprets these results:

> Self-esteem and satisfaction with life can be presumed to depend to greater degree on vocational achievement in relation to aspirations than would feelings of social distrust (personal morale), social withdrawal, and other elements of mental health which are more likely to derive from lifelong influences apart from the job. These latter components might be expected to reflect the direct contribution of education in helping a person at any economic level more effectively come to terms with his world.[42]

The study also shows that education leads to dissatisfaction unless the expected rewards and status are forthcoming.

We have been able to find in Canadian poll data, compiled for this study, further evidence among Canadians of this dissatisfaction. In 1963 a sample was asked, "On the whole would you say that you are satisfied or dissatisfied with the work that you do?" Table 3 shows that for both white collar and blue collar workers, the percentage of those who say that they are satisfied *decreases* with each increase in the level of education. However, among managers the opposite is true: the proportion satisfied with the work they do increases with increases in education.

The implication of this table is that, among white and blue collar workers, education raises the level of expectation higher than their jobs can satisfy. This is especially so among white collar workers, who, as Meltz has shown, often have as much or more education than managers. Since we know that skilled workers are generally satisfied with their jobs,

TABLE 3

MEN SATISFIED WITH WORK

OCCUPATION OF HEAD OF FAMILY	PUBLIC SCHOOL		SECONDARY OR HIGH SCHOOL		MORE THAN HIGH SCHOOL	
	Percentage	Number	Percentage	Number	Percentage	Number
Professional	100.00	1	100.00	2	100.00	20
Managerial	80.00	5	90.91	22	100.00	11
White collar	100.00	3	93.10	29	66.67	9
Blue collar	83.33	60	76.60	47	76.47	17

SOURCE: A reanalysis of 1963 Gallup Poll data from the repository at Carleton University.

if we could break down the statistics in table 3 by the various skill levels within blue collar, we might see that an even greater proportion of semi-skilled workers with a high school education are dissatisfied.

We know that education is also related positively to income levels, and this relationship induces another expectation. The Canadian survey, taken in November 1963, asked, "On the whole would you say that you are satisfied or dissatisfied with your family income?" Of those with more than high school education, 100 per cent of managers, 78 per cent of white collar, and 65 per cent of blue collar workers were satisfied with their family incomes. Since the proportions of those who were satisfied in each occupational group decrease as educational level decreases, it would seem that in fact those with higher education are making more money, even if their status has not improved as much as they expected. On the other hand, we still must recognize that the same level of education seems to offer less financial satisfaction for the blue collar worker than for other groups. (See table 4.)

A similar study by the Survey Research Center in the United States, using the same sort of question, yielded the results shown in table 5.

The U.S. figures also showed that among both white collar and blue collar workers the percentage of people who say that they are very satisfied decreases with increasing levels of education although, at the same time, the primary school groups have the highest percentage of those who say that they are dissatisfied with their incomes. At this income level, it is probably a case of real inadequacy of wages rather than an inadequacy relative to expectation. Among managers, the higher the level of education, the larger the proportion of those who report that

TABLE 4

MEN SATISFIED WITH FAMILY INCOME

OCCUPATION OF HEAD OF FAMILY	PUBLIC SCHOOL		SECONDARY OR HIGH SCHOOL		MORE THAN HIGH SCHOOL	
	Percentage	Number	Percentage	Number	Percentage	Number
Professional	100.00	1	50.00	2	90.00	20
Managerial	80.00	5	77.27	22	100.00	11
White collar	33.33	3	58.62	29	77.78	9
Blue collar	58.33	60	61.70	47	64.71	17

SOURCE: A reanalysis of 1963 Gallup Poll data from the repository at Carleton University.

TABLE 5

SATISFACTION WITH FINANCIAL STATUS AMONG THOSE
WITH MORE THAN HIGH SCHOOL EDUCATION

HIGH SCHOOL OR MORE	Managers and Proprietors (113)	White Collar (84)	Blue Collar (123)
Very satisfied	61%	40%	37%
More or less satisfied	32	43	43
Not satisfied	6	16	19

SOURCE: A reanalysis of data from the 1964 election survey obtained from the Inter-University Consortium for Political Research, University of Michigan, Ann Arbor.

they are very satisfied. The U.S. and the Canadian figures both suggest that it is only at the managerial level that people with a high school education or more have the chance to use it effectively and to gain satisfactory rewards.

Education and Political and Social Attitudes

Political attitudes of individuals or of groups in the society may be expected to be translated into action when the occasion demands, and even to determine what kind of action is likely to be taken. Since unions are political organizations, it is of interest to us to determine whether a rise in educational levels may be expected to affect political attitudes of union members toward union officers and policies. In terms of public policy it may be rewarding to know whether education affects the attitudes of workers toward the government, political parties, and the general society.

Fortunately, there has been a most exhaustive study of political attitudes and their relationship to numerous variables in five nations by Almond and Verba, the results of which were published in 1963 under the title, *The Civic Culture*. The findings with regard to the effects of education on political attitudes are numerous and worth quoting here. These results hold true even when age and occupation are held constant.

It is of great interest, and among the most important facts we discovered, that most of the relationships between education and political orientation are of the first type; i.e., educational groups differ from one another substantially, and in a similar way, in each nation. The manifestations of this cross-national uniformity are the following:

(1) The more educated person is more aware of the impact of government on the individual than is the person of less education.

(2) The more educated individual is more likely to report that he follows politics and pays attention to election campaigns than is the individual of less education.

(3) The more educated individual has more political information.

(4) The more educated individual has opinions on a wider range of political subjects; the focus of his attention to politics is wider.

(5) The more educated individual is more likely to engage in political discussion.

(6) The more educated individual feels free to discuss politics with a wider range of people. Those with less education are more likely to report that there are many people with whom they avoid such discussions.

(7) The more educated individual is more likely to consider himself capable of influencing the government; this is reflected both in responses to questions on what one could do about an unjust law and in respondents' scores on the subjective competence scale.

The above list refers to specifically political orientations, which vary the same way in all five nations. In addition, our evidence shows that:

(8) The more educated individual is more likely to be a member—an active member—of some organization.

(9) The more educated individual is more likely to express confidence in his social environment; to believe that other people are trustworthy and helpful.[43]

The material presented in *The Civic Culture* reveals some striking evidence of the perfect association between level of education and the subjective sense of competence, or the feeling of potency with regard to the world around one, particularly with regard to the political process. These findings, that the more a man is educated the more he is interested in politics, the more he participates, and the more he trusts his fellow man, are obviously significant for governments, but also for unions, because they suggest that in unions involving an educated membership (and as educational levels go up this should include more and more of them), we should expect more active participation on the part of members. The trust in his fellow man makes an educated man more likely to act collectively, and his greater sense of competence is likely to make him feel that he can change union leaders and union policies if they do not suit him. The one possibility which would negate this effect is that unions might fail so miserably to represent workers or to be effective in relations with management that the membership would ignore the union organization and seek redress through the political system itself. The important point is that a worker who is dissatisfied because his position on the job or in society is not as high as his level of education leads him to expect will also feel capable of acting politically to change this state of affairs and will be more likely to do so than his less educated colleagues.

Various Canadian polls, as well as studies of U.S. political attitudes and the Almond study, show that, in general, the educated man tends to be more liberal in his views than a less educated one. For example, the Kraft report of the American Federation of Labor-Congress of Industries Organizations in the United States shows that the greatest amount of criticism concerning various AFL-CIO policy positions was made by the younger workers. Among Canadian blue collar workers, the higher the level of education, the *smaller* the proportion who favour compulsory arbitration, the retention of the death penalty, and the restriction of the picket line to union members in the plant. Also, the higher the level of education, the greater the number who approve bringing thousands of skilled immigrants to Canada.

The differences in attitudes found between educated and less educated people in five nations by the Almond study are already, it would seem, causing trouble within unions.

Another source of intraunion conflict attributable to rising educational levels is that as management and government have become more specialized and complicated, unions have been forced to hire their own experts in order to deal adequately with these groups. One result has been conflict in union leadership between the intellectuals (a word frequently used to mean highly educated) and the missionaries (those whose devotion to the union comes from the heart rather than the head). The intellectuals are often resented as "outsiders" because they have not come up through labour ranks nor experienced the rough battle of organizing the union in the early days, yet their expertise gives them positions of power. Wilensky says that this has been a feature of several serious internal wars in the labour movement in the United States and quotes two instances taken from the CIO Rubberworkers Convention proceedings:

> Delegate Robert Hill: Your thinking on this matter . . . is fantastic. You are a legal mind; you are from Harvard, or Yale, or some other place like the rest of the guys up there, and you don't understand the thinking of the workers.[44]

And from an interview between Harold Wilensky and a staff expert for an unnamed union:

> s.e.: When things were dull, and someone wanted to get a rise out of the crowd, one thing was sure fire: make a speech about how the union has been turned over to a bunch of outsiders in the national office. End it with, "We want to give the Gadgetworkers Union back to the gadgetworkers!" and it'd bring the house down every time. . . .
>
> h.l.w.: Yes, I understand it became a badge of honor to say that you didn't have any education.
>
> s.e.: Yeah, X said he only went through grammar school. He was boasting about it. When Y (factional opponent) stumbled over a word he stopped and said, "I can't even spell it!" What a faker.[45]

In English Canada, the merger of socialists from the old Cooperative Commonwealth Federation Party with unionists from the Canadian Confederation of Labour caused the same kind of conflict, but on ideological rather than generational lines. Horowitz quotes James Kidd of the Sudbury Mine Mill union as saying:

> If the Ontario CCF does not become more of a labour party . . . it will not be a party at all. I think that we are cursed with an excess of professors, lawyers, and other assorted professional people. Too many of the CCF leaders take the attitude that as the CCF is a labour party labour will vote for it even without proper strength on the councils of the party. With so many educated gentlemen who have a habit of tangling themselves up in numerous committees there is no practical approach . . . about all [they] can do is sit around and talk. . . . They are a bunch of old women. . . . The CCF in my opinion should be taken out of the hands of the intellectuals and made more of a union party.[46]

This statement also suggests the same anti-intellectual bent existed among English-Canadian union leaders, at least some of them, and Horowitz confirms that this class and educational conflict was, and still is, reasonably general. In French Canada, however, it is usual for labour leaders to come from the educated élite; thus the division between the leaders and the intellectuals is not apparent.

That union leaders of the older generation, where they are still in control, will have the same anti-intellectual bias found in the U.S. unions by Wilensky is further suggested by the slowness of Canadian unions to employ research staffs. Only the largest of Canadian unions, such as the Steelworkers, the Canadian Union of Public Employees, and the Automobile Workers have recently begun to employ staff experts. As unions face more and more complex negotiations across the table from management staff experts, and as younger, more educated workers reach the decision-making level of labour organizations, this situation is bound to change, if unions are to hold their own at the bargaining table.

An important element of emotional commitment to unionism has in the past been equated with a strong identification with the working class. A reanalysis of the Survey Research Center's 1964 U.S. election survey shows that within all occupational groups, the higher the education, the larger the percentage of people who call themselves middle class. Table 6 shows how the blue collar workers defined themselves in answer to this question:

> There's been a lot of talk these days about different social classes. Most people say they belong to either the middle class or to the working class. Do you think of yourself as being one of these classes? If yes, which one? If no, well, if you have to make a choice, would you call yourself middle or working class?

The majority of the working class still identifies with that class in the United States, but education is eroding this allegiance.

Alford shows that subjective identification of class is strongly associated with party preference (see table 7). In Britain, class voting is high in general (that is, voters consistently vote in terms of their class interests), and 78 per cent of manual workers who consider themselves working class vote Labour, whereas of those who call themselves middle class, only 50 per cent do so. Similarly, among nonmanual workers who call themselves middle class, only 20 per cent vote Labour, but of those who identify with the working class, 52 per cent vote Labour. In the United States, where class voting is low, as it is in Canada, subjective class

TABLE 6

SOCIAL CLASS IDENTIFICATION OF BLUE COLLAR
WORKERS ACCORDING TO THEIR LEVEL OF EDUCATION

CLASS IDENTIFICATION	LEVEL OF EDUCATION		
	Grade School (76)	High School (417)	More than High School (123)
Middle class	10.6%	20.8%	39.6%
Working class	89.1	77.4	57.8

SOURCE: A reanalysis of 1964 U.S. election survey obtained from the Inter-University Consortium for Political Research, University of Michigan, Ann Arbor.

TABLE 7

LABOUR OR DEMOCRATIC PREFERENCE, BY OCCUPATION TYPE AND SUBJECTIVE CLASS IDENTIFICATION, GREAT BRITAIN (1957), UNITED STATES (1952)

PER CENT PREFERRING LABOUR OR DEMOCRATIC PARTIES
*Subjective Class Identification**

Occupation Type	Working Class		Middle Class		Total	
	United States	Great Britain	United States	Great Britain	United States	Great Britain
Manual	59(482)	78(454)	45(143)	50(269)	57(642)	67(737)
Nonmanual	49(191)	52(457)	24(267)	20 (85)	34(480)	24(551)
Index of class voting	+10	+26	+21	+30	+23	+43

SOURCE: BIPO Survey no. 1717, February, 1957, and the Michigan Survey Research Center Survey of the 1952 United States presidential election. Compiled by Robert R. Alford, *Party and Society*, table 11-3, p. 333. Copyright 1963 by Rand McNally & Company, Chicago; reprinted by permission of the publisher.

*The table includes all those as "middle class" who identified themselves as lower middle class, middle class, or upper middle class. Only those specifically calling themselves "working class" are included as such. Discrepancies in the totals are due to omission of persons rejecting the whole idea of social classes or not answering. The total proportion preferring Labour in the British survey was 48 per cent, the total proportion preferring the Democratic Party in the United States survey was 47 per cent.

identification still shows up. Only 45 per cent of manual workers identifying themselves as middle class vote Democratic, compared to 59 per cent if they call themselves working class. Nonmanual, with middle-class identity, vote 24 per cent Democratic, compared to 49 per cent if they identify themselves as working class.[47] These figures suggest that there is a three-step process here. Education raises self-esteem and blurs class consciousness, and the final result is a change in the person's class identification and definition of where his best interests lie.

This change in social class identification might be expected to appear at the polls, but in both the United States and Canada, as Alford has shown, there is little class voting and both tend to place regional, religious, and ethnic interests above class interests. In any case, in the United States, in spite of the rapid rise of general educational levels between 1936 and 1960, the proportion of the population voting for the Democrats (assuming this to be the party of the liberal, working class) and the Republicans (the more conservative, probusiness party) has been little affected. Change over a similar period (1940–61) in Canada shows, however, that the Liberal and the New Democratic parties have lost some ground to Conservatives and Social Credit. Education may account for this trend, but we cannot be sure of this.[48]

Horowitz in *Canadian Labour in Politics* points out that this comparison with the United States may not be a valid way to look at Canadian politics. The New Democratic Party is, he states, the only genuine Left or Labour party, the Liberal party being really a centre party, as demonstrated by "strong indications that the higher strata [of social classes] are more likely than the lower to vote Conservative, the lower strata are more likely than the higher to vote CCF-NDP, and that both are equally attracted to the Liberals."[49] If we accept this point of view, the drift toward the Conservatives would appear even larger.

Summary

We have shown in this section how rising levels of education are an integral part of technologically advancing economy and, at the same time, produce certain strains within unions and in the society. These strains are caused partly by conflict of views between the educated and the less educated and partly by a discrepancy between what people expect when they achieve a high level of education and what is actually forthcoming, although fortunately this is not true in general. Where it is true, however, the educated worker has a greater interest in and feeling of capacity to act politically to change things, through the union or through the larger society, than the less educated worker. We suggest that, whatever the stresses, rising levels of education have produced more people who are potentially better able and more willing to participate in democratic processes, whether in the union, the factory, or the nation. Fortunately or unfortunately, this does not necessarily mean more peaceful industrial or political relations.

As Victor Allen has pointed out: "the newly emerging strike prone groups are the draughtsmen, schoolteachers and clerks. In the past the apprentice-skilled craftsmen were always better educated than other manual workers and at the same time were more effective in their industrial action. More effective and equitable educational and training facilities for shop-stewards might only result in better organized strikes or more sophisticated strike methods."[50]

4

Technological Change

Although there have been affluent individuals or groups in the past, affluent *societies* are not possible until a high level of technological development has been reached. One of the most salient features of technological development is that it involves continuous, unending change. And here we do not mean simply that production methods may change from one generally accepted and stable one to another equally widespread and stable, or that the social relationships on and off the job which technical changes give rise to are only a move from one fixed point to another. What seems to characterize the age of automation and mass consumption is a state of "fluidity," in which a man may expect in his own lifetime to change his job, to be retrained, to change his social and geographic environment, his friends, his community, his standard of living, even his beliefs and values, not once but perhaps many times. And he knows that he can only dimly guess what life will be like for his children. We do not have to go back to feudal times to appreciate the qualitative difference between life under these circumstances and life under conditions of relative stability. Even at the turn of the century, very few of the above conditions would have held true for the average man.

Technological change and automation in particular will greatly influence the environment of the emerging worker. Such developments and the process of continually improving productivity per man hour, which advanced technology represents, are both the cause of worker affluence and the result of economic activities of an advanced and affluent society. A highly developed technology presupposes the existence of a large enough body of trained scientists, technicians, managers, and workers to invent, plan, operate, and service its factories, plus consumers who are trained and educated to want and use its products, and, finally, a group of people trained to repair and service the products. The number of trained people required to produce, use, and service the automobile, to take just one obvious example, becomes most apparent when one imagines trying to produce one in an underdeveloped society. In short, for automation to exist we must have the physical capital to invest in expensive machinery, the human capital to invent, plan, produce, service, and use it, and the certainty that the ever-increasing volume of goods produced will be consumed at a profitable level in ever-expanding markets.

Technological change will also influence the relations between labour and management, since these relations are a function of the work environment as well as of the larger social environment, and attitudes toward each other, expressed in grievances or collective bargaining, may be formed in either place. It is important therefore to understand how the daily contacts between workers and management are changing and what we may expect in the future. It is also important to understand the effects of technological change in the context of the larger society where industrial relations become public and of public concern.

Here we will be primarily concerned with changes in relations of worker to worker and worker to manager within the industrial plant. In the second chapter, we showed the growing importance of the white collar and service workers in the labour force of mass consumption economies. We know that teachers, civil servants, nurses, and technicians are joining unions and negotiating collective contracts. Furthermore, we believe that the white collar worker will increasingly share the work experience of the blue collar worker as automation in the office proceeds, and that we can safely assume that, in concentrating on industrial experience and industrial workers, we have a good index of trends in the world of work and labour-management relations.

Let us accept, then, that the existence of a trend toward increasingly automatic factories is evidence of an affluent, mass consumption society and of a society most of whose members have a rather high level of education or technical training. What effects does such an environment have on the attitudes of workers and management?

The New Work Environment

Automation, or continuous process production, in which a greater and greater proportion of the work is performed, regulated, and controlled by machines rather than by men, is the latest stage in changing production technology. Its introduction has caused increased productivity comparable to, although not as great as, the introduction of mass production in the twenties.[1] This process has not had, however, quite the effects originally expected, since completely automated plants are rare, and most industries that are automated at all tend to be so only in certain sections of their operations. Machines do not yet exist to take over every kind of work, and in some cases it appears to be inefficient or uneconomical to replace men with machines.[2]

However, the degree of automation will determine the work and social changes experienced by the workers. Insofar as generalizations can be made, Bright finds that, whereas setup and maintenance men encounter an *increase* in skill and responsibility requirements where automation is low or medium, further automation tends to reduce these requirements except for a few positions. The work of engineers and technicians is narrowed and is concentrated on a few specializations, with the exception of research and high level planning operations. The production workers' jobs require progressively less dexterity, less knowledge of art or theory, less experience, less physical effort, less judgement, and less decision-making, and the workers have a diminished control of the work pace as automation becomes more intensive and extensive.[3]

> While control is in the hands of the individual, skill and judgment are the premium characteristics. As the machine takes over guidance, knowledge of the machine regulation becomes more important. And as controls become more and more comprehensive in prescribing the operating action, skill and knowledge requirements increase, and then start to diminish. Judgment grows less important since the controls take over decisions. However, responsibility grows because misdirected action has great impact or can do great damage. At some point, as the controls become more sensitive and responsive to the requirements of the operating environment and the task, the machine assumes responsibility just as it has already assumed skill, knowledge, and judgment requirements. Thus, increasing mechanization modifies the worker's contributions and also changes their economic value.[4]

There is some argument about whether technological change necessarily brings unemployment, but the weight of evidence seems to be that some kinds of skill do disappear, that individuals and even groups may be downgraded or shifted to other kinds of work, and that "the major factor of displacement seems to be the reduced manpower requirements of the A-unit (an automated factory or part thereof). At present, the effects are not obvious because of the slow pace of automation and perhaps the constant pressure of labour unions. In order to diminish resistance, management has planned manpower reduction policies so that vested interests would be the least hurt. This involved first the gradual elimination of temporary help, and, as a second step, the limitation of new hiring. Thus, after a time the total payroll shrinks to the desired proportions."[5] We might add that efforts to retire older workers early and to postpone the age at which young people appear on the labour market through demanding higher educational qualifications serve the same purpose. Although statistically it may be difficult to prove that automation produces unemployment,[6] it is perfectly clear that some jobs do disappear and some groups do suffer as a result of technological change, the disappearance of the blacksmith being perhaps the simplest well-known example.

In Canada, between 1957 and 1961, the Department of Labour made a study of five industries in an attempt to estimate the effects of technological change on manpower, as regards both its quantity and quality. The findings show that in these plants the use of semiautomatic and automatic machines resulted in a reduction in the number of semiskilled and unskilled workers and an increase in the demand for maintenance workers. At the same time, there was a large increase in office or clerical workers, including machine operators, but an overall fall in employment of 3 per cent. Since maintenance workers tend to be more carefully selected in automated or semiautomated plants because of the high cost of the machinery and of breakdowns, and since, also, the number of clerical and administrative employees goes up, one can see that the "quality" of the labour force also rises with automation. If Bright is correct, however, this was true only in Canada, at that time, under those average conditions of automation for those five industries, and cannot be generalized.

Although the amount of physical distance between workers varies with the degree of automation and the kind of plant, there is a tendency for there to be greater physical distance between work stations, and less contact between workers in automated than in preautomated factories—in some cases only telephone contact is possible. This isolation, some workers feel, is detrimental to a desired work environment.

Investigators in the United States and in England found that workers complain that they have fewer opportunities for promotion in the continuous process system.[7] Floyd Mann reasons that: "With smaller work forces, fewer job classes, fewer levels of supervision and increasingly complex technical work environments, many workers feel the promotional ladders they had planned to climb are shortened or shattered. There is less opportunity for advancement into supervisory positions; career lines are often destroyed. Accumulated skills may be wiped out, and requirements substituted which the worker does not have the education to acquire."[8]

Wage losses are often reported in the beginning by production workers, especially if they are on piece rates or productivity incentive schemes, because until they learn to operate the new machines they may actually make less. During this early stage of adaptation to more automated machinery, the men feel that the job requires much greater mental alertness and they are keenly sensitive to the greater responsibility. They believe that the tension and strain are much greater than in the older methods, where on mass production lines each man was responsible for a much smaller portion of the process and a mistake was less costly than under continuous process production.

Management, too, has its problems, for as the structure of the production system changes, so also must the structure of authority and responsibility. Relationships tend to become more formal, the function of management grows in importance with technical change, and more recruits are needed with specialized qualifications. "It becomes more difficult than before to rise from the ranks and there is a possibility, at least in the transitional phase, of rivalry among groups who differ in function or personal backgrounds."[9] Coordination and control within the ranks of an increasingly complex management become more difficult. Scott suggests that "the trend toward specialization may in time lead to the creation of a management group composed entirely of professional men, who are formally recruited and trained and who possess definite qualifications."[10]

There is considerable difference of opinion as to whether supervision is better or worse, but in any case it is clearly different. More technical knowledge is required of the foreman or supervisor; he is responsible for a larger segment of the productive process and, often, for more men. Many workers feel that supervision is more impersonal and, particularly at the early stages, more exacting. Durand, in a study of French workers, describes how the hierarchies of skill and responsibility flatten, since the mistake of the lowest paid operator may be as costly and as difficult to remedy as that of the highest ranking, and supervisor and operator alike function on the basis of plans handed down from technicians in planning departments.[11]

Sociopsychological Reaction to Technical Change

It can be argued that the differences in craftsmanship or unit production, mass production, and continuous process production, which are only stages on a continuum of technical efficiency, are, in human terms, differences so great as to constitute diversified social environments, to foster various attitudes toward fellow workers, management, unions, and the society at large, and to change the meaning of work and leisure. In this section, we will explain some of these differences and worker reactions to them. At the same time, it is important to remember that all three types of production are present simultaneously in the society and even in a given plant. The new work environment of automation is important because it predicts the future, but worker (and management and staff) attitudes will vary with the *degree* of technical advance represented by their predominant work experience and with the length of time they have been in it.

Men's attitudes toward technological change, or specifically automation, vary with occupational level. The staff, who identify with management's interest in efficiency and whose ranks may actually grow as a result of automation, are inclined to be enthusiastic about installation of automated machinery. Skilled workers and white collar workers are likely to feel that, relative to other workers, they may suffer a demotion, and their skills may lose status. They see that even though they may lose nothing in wages or status in an absolute sense, they lose relatively to production workers whose position improves. They may, on the other hand, be in greater demand, as maintenance workers become more important. The least enthusiastic about prospects of automation in their factories are the production workers, who are most threatened by loss of both their jobs and opportunity for promotion. As Scott found, "the higher the occupational status, the greater is the support for technical change in the face of unpleasant social consequences (such as unemployment) the greater is the support for the rights of management and the less is the approval of union claims."[12]

However, workers' attitudes change as they get used to the new plant.

Most surveys show that workers begin by being suspicious and anxious about the new machinery and techniques. These reactions are based on a realistic fear that they may lose their jobs (or that someone will), or be downgraded, or lose old skills which may have required a lifetime to perfect and on which their prestige among fellow workers is based. If they are skilled workers, their use of these skills may have been an important part of their work satisfaction. Older workers worry about whether they will be able to perform on the new and unfamiliar machinery at such high speeds, and show a reluctance to learn new methods.

Walker found that the reactions of men in an automated U.S. steel plant changed as they adapted themselves to the new process. Interviews conducted in the early stages, one and two years after the introduction of automated machinery, indicated that workers found the isolation from other workers, the increased tension and responsibility, the tighter supervision (which tends to occur until supervisors and workers get used to the new process), the lack of satisfactory pay increases, and the loss of past skills to be sources of dissatisfaction. On the other hand, after three years, the same men reported that they were, in general, pleased with the change. They liked the variety of their jobs, the responsibility, the sense of understanding their part in the whole process as related to other specific parts, the improved physical setup (cleaner, better lighting), the reduction of hard manual work, and the status they enjoyed in the community as a result of being in the most modern factory or part of it. Also, they had mastered the process, which meant fewer stoppages and breakdowns; this resulted in higher productivity, and thus, higher wages.[13] Bright found the same pattern and comments that, "Automation, by spreading the worker's station over a greater span of the production activity, is a definite contributor to job enlargement and its benefits for the individual."[14]

There are, however, certain universal reactions to the new work environment that do not vary with the time of exposure. With affluence and technological advance, workers tend to develop a sense of greater equalitarianism and an instrumental or extrinsic view of their work—sometimes even a considerable personal detachment from it.

Trend toward Equalitarianism

The tendency toward greater equalitarianism seems to be a result of several factors. Two important ones are that automation results in fewer job classifications with less difference between the highest and lowest as to wages or responsibility, and that new, more easily learned skills tend to replace old skills.

Walker interviewed workers in a newly installed, continuous seamless pipe mill at the Lorain works of U.S. Steel as to whether they thought they had more chance for promotion in the new mill than in the old. One worker compared the new mill to the old in terms which demonstrate the flattening of job hierarchies: "The jobs are now all about the same. On the old mills, you could go from a job class 4 up to a job class 20, and there were about thirty jobs on the mill. On Number 4 everything is around job class 9 to class 16 and there are not as many of them."[15]

Durand found that, among French workers, flattening of job hierarchies was also reflected in the informal relationships among them. Less respect was accorded on the basis either of skill or authority, and skilled workers, formerly enjoying prestige because they possessed skills difficult to acquire, were called "the old ones" and were sneered at because they did not know how to run the new machines.[16]

One of the most striking proofs of this equalitarian trend is furnished by a comparative report on six national studies of workers' adjustment to technical change published by the Organization for European Economic Cooperation. In the Netherlands and in France a "reversal of the élite" was found to have occurred in the automated steel mills studied. Young men with lower wages had received more wage increases than others, and 40 per cent of those in the highest paid group before the change had an actual decrease in wages. The report states: "The explanation for this trend seems to lie in a change of emphasis from qualifications based on long experience on the job to formal educational qualification. In Holland, this has clearly happened. Workers with more than primary education have received more wage increases and less wage decreases, irrespective of age, than those whose education ceased at the primary level. But in France too, the same pattern seems to have been repeated."[17] This pattern was not found in Britain, where the seniority principle was the mechanism for selection and promotion. However, the report points out that: "In addition, differences in the educational system must also be taken into account, for formal educational qualifications were rarely possessed by the steel-workers in the British firm."

There is less difference in the wages, prestige, and responsibility not only among workers, but also between workers and their supervisors. This is important not only for its effect in equalization on the job, but because it may be reflected in broader social attitudes.

Change in Meaning of Work

The second universal and important result of technological change, which seems to be true for both mass production and continuous process production, is that work, once considered one of the principle sources of man's satisfaction, his status and prestige, and the centre of his important social relations, changes its meaning. It now becomes simply a means to an end, that is, making a living and, of course, the higher the standard the better.

We have already mentioned that, as compared to mass production assembly lines, the continuous process plant creates physically greater distances among workers as well as somewhat more formal relationships among workers and between workers and supervisors. The breakup of the time-honoured work team and the social meaning with which it was presumed to invest work has not turned out to be as seriously disrupting as expected. Even more significant has been the futility of trying to make work as intrinsically meaningful and satisfying for the assembly-line worker as it once was for the craftsman, and in some respects this alienation of man from his work is carried a step farther with automation. Dubin suggested in 1955 that three out of four workers in three industrial plants in the middle west of the United States did not regard work as their central life interest, and did not make nor seek their most important social relationships on the job.[18] This has been confirmed by Goldthorpe and Lockwood's study of three technically advanced plants in Luton, England, which shows that workers have an almost totally instrumental view of their work and do not have, or particularly want, close personal relationships with their fellow workers. "To the extent that work is defined as a mandatory form of activity and as one engaged in simply as a means to an end, the work-place will not be regarded as a milieu appropriate or favourable to the development of highly rewarding primary relationships. . . . So far as work goes, emotionally significant experiences and 'significant others' will tend neither to be looked for nor, thus, to be greatly missed in their absence."[19]

Work, then, has changed its connotation since the days of craft work, and men, at least at the blue collar level, are not likely to invest themselves or their egos in the performance of the kind of tasks required in mass assembly or continuous process industries. Dubin finds that the worker now turns his interests and involvements to family, community, and other nonwork areas.[20] He still has sufficient attachment to his job to be dependable and efficient, because it is the means of his real satisfactions. Goldthorpe and his associates feel that such attitudes may be adaptive to the increasing impersonality of work places and supervision.[21] Naville believes that the modern worker's detachment from his job may free him for wider, more creative pursuits, and that it is totally useless to expect a man to satisfy his deeper needs from work over which he has so little direct control.[22]

We should ask at this point what the attitudes of workers would be if they had more control. A. H. Maslow's hierarchy of needs theory suggests that, whereas man is originally motivated to work largely in order to obtain food, clothes, and housing, these physical needs, once satisfied, are no longer motivators and a next level of need will become insistent. In other words, man works in order to satisfy his needs, but new needs continually arise to replace already satisfied ones. According to the Maslow hierarchy, physiological needs are followed by social needs, that is, needs for association, acceptance, for friendship and love. After these have been fulfilled, a man will work to satisfy egotistic needs for self-esteem, for achievement, competence, and knowledge, and in order to increase his reputation and gain status, appreciation, and respect. Finally, when a man feels he has a reasonable amount of self-esteem and status, he may work for self-fulfillment—to realize his potentialities, to create.[23] Efforts by social scientists to verify this hypothesis have introduced certain caveats which may be appropriate here. Notably, that when progression through this list of reasons for working is halted at any stage, people tend to seek exaggerated compensation at the lower level and/or attempt to seek the denied satisfaction outside work. Furthermore, Blauner's comparisons of different kinds of industries in his *Alienation and Freedom* make it clear that industrial processes offer a wide variety of work experience, ranging from the assembly line, where alienation seems clear and job satisfactions meagre, to unit operations where higher levels of needs are sometimes satisfied. Goldthorpe's study also confirms that work experience varies with industrial process, in spite of his general conclusion that workers have largely extrinsic view of their work.[24]

In any case, Dubin's view that self-fulfillment in work may be a dead issue leaves many social scientists, including us, uneasy, since they feel that if this is so in our society, it is a serious matter and needs remedying. All the more so, in light of Kornhauser's evidence that "favorable or unfavorable job feelings [carry over] to produce corresponding feelings in other sectors of life." He finds no evidence that "men who are more dissatisfied in work find extra enjoyment away from work, or conversely, that those dissatisfied at home and leisure manage especially to find satisfaction in work."[25]

Blauner believes, and we tend to agree, that work in our society remains the single most important life activity for most people, that there is continual interaction between the quality of one's work life and one's nonwork life.[26] To this we would add that it is morally unacceptable to accept a definition in which some people (workers) are able to be creative only in their leisure life, while other people are capable of self-fulfillment in work *and* leisure.

Technological Change and White Collar Occupations

Automation has also come to the office, and the clerical worker has, with the semiskilled worker, been the group whose work process has been most affected by technological change. Clerical work is also one of the fastest growing occupational categories in all advanced countries; in fact in the United States by 1960, white collar workers outnumbered blue collar workers.[27] Professional, technical, and managerial groups are also growing and are included in white collar or nonmanual occupations. It is primarily the clerical workers with whom we are concerned here.

Even as early as the fifties, C. Wright Mills was saying of white collar work: "Mechanized and standardized work, the decline of any chance for the employee to see and understand the whole operation, the loss of any chance, save for a very few, for private contact with those in authority, these form the model of the future."[28] Although David Lockwood, writing about the same time in Britain, found the rationalization and mechanization of office work less advanced, as one might expect, he does comment that large scale organizations, such as the civil service, railways, and banks employ thousands of white collar employees, and the ensuing highly bureaucratic relationship, in which the individual worker is related to his fellows and his organization only through uniform and impersonal standards, represents a vast change from the small, private commercial or industrial firm wherein the clerk or stenographer was in daily personal contact with higher levels of management and physically separated from the production process. The status and self-conception which the white collar worker enjoyed was partly, at least, a result of this contact with management or the owner: the clerk might have been the lowest member of the middle class, but he was definitely, through income, dress, aspirations, education, and association identified with it.[29]

The lower levels of white collar work are becoming in many ways indistinguishable from factory work. With automation, factories and offices are almost equally clean, and supervision is as impersonal in one as in the other. Workers in both places can and sometimes do wear white shirts, are machine operators, need and have about the same educational attainment level, and there is little if any difference in pay levels. There are, however, two differences: the clerical worker is female (74.1 per cent of them were female in Canada in 1961)[30]; and, while automation has brought a rise in status and income for the manual worker, it has meant a relative loss in these things for the nonmanual worker. The large, open, modern office with the banks of IBM machines, the computers, calculators, and duplicating machines, the dictating machines which have made shorthand almost obsolete and contact with the boss unnecessary, the beltline methods, where each girl only punches certain cards, or types and assembles certain kinds of material, produce in the clerical worker many of the same feelings of frustration and meaninglessness in work which Chinoy found in the automobile workers, as we shall see later. As C. Wright Mills observed about office production-line plans and techniques:

> These techniques and ways of reasoning have been long established in office-management circles and are identical with the reasoning found in factory-management circles. Their advance in offices, however, is still uneven, being perhaps in the first instance, limited by the size of the office . . . but offices continually become larger and, as they do, changes occur: personal telephone calls, smoking during office hours, visits from personal friends, and handling of personal mail are restricted, while mechanization and social rationalization— including rest periods, rest rooms, and hospital plans—increase.[31]

Thus, we see that the same changes which give factory workers a sense of improvement in the conditions and satisfaction of work, and in their prestige away from work, represent for the office workers a loss in the control, the variety, the intrinsic interest, and the status which the job had formerly offered. They may, furthermore, even be getting less pay, relatively, to blue collar workers. All these factors are of considerable importance in the unionization of clerical workers. In an eight-nation study of white collar unions, the following point was made by Sturmthal:

> Since white-collar unions represent the lower white-collar grades to a larger extent than they represent the upper grades, their members are

more likely to be among those whose wage advantage compared with blue-collar workers has been shrinking. A hint of confirmation for this inference can perhaps be found in the fact that most white-collar unions have complained about the compression of the wage structure and the reduction of traditional differentials between blue- and white-collar workers. One of the main objectives of the Australian white-collar unions has been to re-establish these differentials. The same applies to Austrian, French and German white-collar unions and, probably, to many others.[32]

What is of greatest importance to our study, however, is that, except for this sense of loss of status and income, the nature of the work experience, the educational level, the consumption patterns, and even many of the aspirations of the lower level of the white collar group can be considered to be increasingly similar to that of the affluent factory worker. Thus, for our purpose, the clerical worker should be included as a sub-group of the emerging worker.

Management Changes

Management, of necessity, has also changed with technological development. Managers are better educated, in general, than they were twenty years ago, before the sharp rise in both affluence and educational levels began. Increasing automation or other levels of technological advance have made it necessary for management to be able to organize men of widely different skills and levels of authority on a vast scale. This demands specialized scientific and professional personnel involved in the technical aspects of research and production, as well as human relations specialists: the psychologist, the sociologist, the personnel man, and the medical and safety specialists, who concern themselves with the motivations, problems, and satisfactions of the men who work in the given industry. Their activities must mesh with the structure of responsibility and authority to get the work done and to this end, management must also organize workers, foremen, and superintendents. Peter Drucker maintains that this skill of organization is a recent development of great importance, not only to industrial relations but to the society at large.

The new organizing capacity creates a middle-class society of men who are professionals in their work but rank as employees, managerial in their responsibility but middle-class in their outlook, expectations, rewards.

This new organizing ability has already created a new social reality. It has given us a new leadership group and a new leadership function: the employed professional manager. . . . It creates a new social problem—the integration of the professional man, both specialists and managers, into the organization—which bids fair to become *the* social question of the twentieth century.[33]

Automation may change the structure of management itself. Ida Moos, in a study of nineteen organizations in San Francisco, found evidence that the introduction of electronic data processing in the offices of these firms has turned the EDP technicians into a new élite. This group, because of their ability to provide up-to-the-minute facts, reports, and analyses of information, is replacing middle management, who used to gather such information and to establish goals and policy—in twice the time and with half the accuracy. Miss Moos finds that these EDP executives are concerned only with efficiency; they do not try to fit into the organization and are not the least interested in the human side of management. "Ignoring all the ground rules of established organizational behavior, it [the EDP department] bypasses channels and cuts across departmental lines—all for the purpose of enhanced efficiency."[34] She notes that personnel work is being handled more and more by computers and even vice-presidents are bypassed, and that such functions as procurement, production, and sales are being turned over to machines. This evidence, of course, raises the possibility that the march of technology may eventually make all men equal in their work, except for a tiny number of thinkers and data programmers. In the foreseeable future, however, it could be that in many automated plants and offices, jobs in middle management, like clerical jobs, will fall in status and compensation, and the technical experts will step into the resulting gap and become the most prestigious group in industry next to top management. On the other hand, this may be an exaggerated view of the capacities of the computer. The importance of Miss Moos' analysis is that it suggests that managers, like white collar workers of the lower levels, may begin to experience loss of status and relative income in their work. In the community, educational gaps between the various strata of society are narrowing (in the foreseeable future, education will be a continuous process for everyone), and standard consumption patterns further erase social distinction. Under the circumstances, it will be increasingly obvious to workers that management's claim to the sole right of decision-making on the job is not based on superior training or capability. We may suppose that management will, in many cases, try to hold on to traditional prerogatives, even though they are no longer based on real distinctions, and that workers will reject its right to keep sole control of the organization of work. We wish to note that so far we cannot visualize that there will not be a need for top management, and it may be that industrial decision-making might simply be concentrated in fewer and fewer hands, thus making a great social distance between this ruling group and the rest of a plant population. Certainly, this discussion should not be taken to negate the earlier statement of the increasing importance of skillful management in complex automatic and semiautomatic plants. But we do not know where the upper limits of routinization of skills lies, how much homogenization of status can or will occur, and how many decisions there are that cannot be made, efficiently, by machines. Until these limits have been reached, the stress and dislocation previously felt only by blue collar workers faced with technological change will be shared now by white collar workers and management. Before the seemingly inexorable march of the machine, we are all equal.

Summary

In this chapter, we have shown that technological change is producing a work environment in which, although the work is pleasanter and offers greater scope and variety for the blue collar worker, and certainly higher incomes, the old hierarchies of skill and authority are reduced or sometimes disappear. The worker experiences a greater sense that he is equal to any other man, but at the same time there is nowhere to go in improving his position in life. Chances of promotion are much smaller, his control over the production process and the skill required to do his work continually diminish, and his relations to fellow workers and supervisors become more impersonal and remote. It becomes difficult to satisfy either his achievement desires or his need for recognition and prestige within the work situation. He therefore turns his creative urges, his ambition, his need for social support and recognition to his private and community world. His work loses most of its emotional and psychological meaning and becomes the means by which he can meet these needs outside of work. Affluence offers the means to achieve recognition, approval of his reference group, a sense of mobility and, hopefully, a creativity, denied by the job. Meanwhile, because change is continuous, workers are continually threatened by loss of their jobs or their skills. A certain detachment from the job and a corresponding investment of self in a "style of life" facilitate the acceptance of this situation.

It must be noted, however, that this situation is not a desirable one.

As automation proceeds, as industry and society become more complex, what we need from workers is no longer their muscles or even their time. What is needed is their responsible, problem-solving involvement. This is not forthcoming from men who find work only a means to other ends. Even if, as Goldthorpe and his associates maintain, such involvement is not necessary for organizational functioning, we believe that rising educational levels, participation in mass consumption norms, as well as changing technology will produce among the workers rising expectations and demands for control and self-fulfillment in all areas of life.

Goldthorpe correctly asserts that too much emphasis has been placed on the work situation as the sole determinant of worker attitudes toward work, whereas the attitudes a man *brings* to his work about its meaning to him may be equally important. We agree. It is precisely because we see the general trend toward equalitarianism, occurring in experiences both inside and outside of work, as producing a different definition of self, a different expectation of what work and life ought to mean, that we expect that workers will not long accept meaningless jobs, even if they are well paid. Dubin's study of man's alienation from his work was made in 1955 and did not include continuous process production. Goldthorpe's study made in 1963–64 could hardly show the effects of high levels of mass education, since Britain is behind the United States and Canada in this, and of the workers studied 85 per cent had left school at age fourteen or before.[35]

5

Labour Mobility

So far, we can see in the mass consumption society the ever-changing interrelationship among several factors: technological development, which leads to affluence, which in turn leads to the ability and willingness to purchase the durable goods associated with a high standard of living, and education, which leads to more technological development, more affluence, and a capacity to foresee a wider range of opportunities, thus developing higher individual aspirations. Also, we have noted that being able to live as well as the next man tends to erode an individual's respect for social distinctions, at least for those that relegate him to an inferior station. The worker, at least in material ways, can feel himself equal to anyone else. And as he achieves higher levels of education, he believes that he has a right to expect to improve his status in his work-life, too, and perhaps also his social prestige. A mass consumption society, then, creates an environment where mobility, both economic and social, becomes possible and expected.

It is important, therefore, to know to what extent a particular national economy is able to meet these mobility aspirations, since frustration of what people believe to be legitimate aims often leads to conflict, economic or political. And here we would argue that it is the *belief* in equality of opportunity that is most important in maintaining the optimism so necessary to citizens in a democratic, mass consumption society. People need to feel that they are part of a fluid society where movement in any direction is never blocked except by lack of skills, and that the society encourages the development of skills for everyone able and willing to learn them. Just as it is the *sense* of political potency, even if not exercised, which is associated with confidence in a political system, so we maintain that it is the *sense* of being able to move to a better job, whether one does or not, which is most important in developing the faith in the economy that leads a worker to invest himself or his income in it.

Job mobility is of three kinds. Occupational or social mobility is the ability and willingness to move from one occupation to another and to move up or down in the scale of occupational hierarchies. Geographic mobility involves the ability and willingness of individuals to move from one location to another in response to job opportunities. Technical mobility is the ability to learn new skills and adjust to changes in the production process. Obviously, all three types of mobility are important to the individual's sense of "getting ahead," and all presuppose, not only willingness to change on the part of individuals, but also the existence of job opportunities and the means by which individuals can take advantage of them. There must be a job in the next town, or a position open in the same occupation with another company, or a different kind of job at a higher or lower status. The economy might, also, be demanding more and different kinds of technical proficiencies, such as more clerks and fewer labourers.

Changes in Labour Force Composition

Perhaps the most important mobility that has occurred in the mass consumption society is attributable to a change in the composition of the labour force.

In Canada, between 1931 and 1961, agricultural occupations dropped from 28.8 per cent of the labour force to 10.5 per cent; labourers experienced the second largest decline (after agriculture)—from the third ranking occupation group in 1931 to the ninth in 1961; clerical workers doubled their percentage of the labour force; and manufacturing and construction occupations had taken over from agricultural workers as the largest occupational group. Professionals also made large gains. This group moved from 6.1 per cent of the labour force in 1931 to 10.3 per cent in 1961—an increase of 2.8 per cent as compared to 2.4 per cent for clerical workers. The female participation in the labour force increased by 10 per cent, mostly in clerical, commercial, and financial occupations, with a surprising increment in agriculture, due to the increasing mechanization of agriculture. The number of males in the labour force between the ages of fourteen and twenty-four and over sixty-five years declined.[1]

This last change, common to the United States and other technologically advanced economies, is caused by prolonged compulsory education, by rising educational requirements for job entry, and by the availability of married women, who are better trained and have more work experience than many adolescents, and who will take the kind of lowly paid or part-time jobs previously held by youths. The decline in the number of employed older men is, at least partly, a result of technological unemployment and/or early retirement plans intended to ease men out of jobs which are disappearing because of technological change.[2]

Summarizing the changes listed above, we can say that as of 1961, in Canada, the managerial, professional, clerical, commercial, and financial occupations accounted for 39.7 per cent of the labour force as compared to 24.5 per cent in 1931, most of this change having taken place since 1941. This compares to 22 per cent in manufacturing and construction and 13 per cent in mining, farming, and other extractive industries in 1961. In 1931, only 16 per cent of the labour force was engaged in manufacturing and construction, while extractive industries employed 32.6 per cent of the working group. It should be noted, however, that employment in manufacturing and construction, with slight ups and downs, is growing at a diminishing rate, so that we can expect that the tertiary sector will shortly exceed employment in manufacturing and construction. It is clear that in Canada the labour force distribution is that typical of a mass consumption society: fewer workers in agriculture and primary industries, more in manufacturing, with white collar and professional groups growing the fastest of all.[3]

Speaking of what these changes mean to the United States, Peter Drucker has said:

> For the first time in our history—or indeed in the history of any country—managerial, professional, and technical employees have become the largest group in our work force. They not only outnumber all other white collar groups, but they have even overtaken manual working groups, especially the machine workers.
>
> Equally significant, for the first time in our history, and again for the first time in the history of any country, people with a high degree of

education—that is, people who have finished high school—constitute more than half our total labor force, including those employed in agriculture.

This trend is certain to accelerate sharply. The number of managerial, professional and technical employees is growing at the rate of 10 per cent each year—three times as fast as the total population. . . . Here is a basic change in the structure of this country and of our economy.[4]

The importance of this trend for a study of mobility is that it shows clearly that the labour force is moving toward occupations of higher prestige, since, in general, the expanding occupations are those of higher prestige and the contracting ones (agriculture, labourers) are of lower prestige. There exist then more and more openings at the middle and higher levels. People will believe that they can improve their positions if they want to, and many of them actually have, as the growth curve shows. Just as the economy has raised the income levels for almost all workers, so it has also raised the prestige level of most of the jobs available.

Occupational and Social Mobility

The general raising of the level of the occupational structure does not necessarily mean, however, that an individual has a better chance of achieving a higher social status than his father had, or that he can go from rags to riches any easier than his father could have. In fact, the evidence is that this kind of individual social mobility has not changed much over the long term and varies little from country to country. There are even those who hypothesize that this kind of mobility may be antithetical to general economic advancement.[5]

Berman, as well as Lipset and Bendix, has shown that the degree or rate of intergenerational social mobility in the United States has changed very little over time and is only slightly greater than that found in various European countries.[6] It is a difficult business to compare a son's occupational status and mobility with his father's (the method usually used to estimate social mobility over time), especially when social and monetary values are changing, and it is not our task to assess such techniques. However, it is important for us to note that Lipset and Bendix, who have done probably the most comprehensive work on the subject of social mobility, came to the conclusion, generally accepted by other authors, that the most important social dividing line is that between the manual and non-manual occupations. Above and below this line, movement is fairly free, but across it movement is rarer and often unstable. The most frequently employed means of crossing this line is by starting a small business of one's own. These authors attribute what upward intergenerational mobility there is to the expansion of the nonmanual sector of the labour force. They continue, "However, most sons of urban dwellers have not changed their class position, as defined by a shift across the manual-nonmanual line, and approximately 10 per cent of them have fallen in status. About 80 per cent of this group have either not significantly improved their class position (from manual to non-manual status) or have declined in position as compared to their fathers."[7]

One of the few studies made of intergenerational occupational mobility in Canada was made in Quebec by Rocher and de Jocas. The comparison was made between the mobility rates of English-speaking sons and French-speaking sons in relation to the occupational status of their fathers. They found that the concentration of English-speaking fathers and sons was in the white collar, professional, and managerial occupations and that manual workers' sons tended to take jobs as white collar workers. French Canadians, on the other hand, were concentrated in the unskilled labour category and their sons, if they moved up, became skilled workers. There was evidence not only of greater mobility among English-speaking sons, but also that the difference seemed to be growing. The increase in the *proportion* of French-Canadian sons in white collar occupations is not nearly so great as that for the English-speaking sons.[8] This difference is subject, obviously, to various interpretations, but it is worth noting here that it is precisely what one would expect in comparing any affluent, mass consumption group or economy with a nonaffluent, traditional group or economy. Until very recently, in Quebec the educational system, the social system, and the value system of French Canada were in general not geared to mobility, to technological change, or to modern consumption norms. As Porter says: "Because of differences in wealth and education within the French-Canadian society, particularly because secondary education was until the 1960's based on private fee-paying schools, Quebec was even more out of the general North American value-pattern of social equality than the rest of Canada."[9]

Whatever may be the case with regard to intergenerational mobility, there seems to be no doubt about the experience of the individual worker *during his own lifetime*. The Palmer study of occupational mobility in six U.S. cities was the most extensive and intensive survey made of the problem. Dubin quotes a Jaffe and Carleton study which, using the material from the Palmer study to estimate *intragenerational* mobility, discovered that for all occupational groups taken together, the chances are better than one in two (55.51 per cent) that a person will end his working life in a higher occupation than the one in which he started. The odds are one in five (20.14 per cent) that no change will be made to either a higher or lower occupation during the working-life history. In sum, three out of every four members of the labour force in the United States will be as well or better off when they leave the labour market as they were when they entered. American workers not only move frequently from job to job, and from industry to industry, but the majority also "get ahead" in the process.[10]

Workers, incidentally, do not have exalted ambitions, and their definitions of advancement and occupational mobility are often modest. Reynolds found that, "the typical worker's conception of 'promotion' is a very limited one. . . . Few workers aspire to office jobs in the company, or to foremanships, or even to skilled maintenance work. Their aspirations are focused on a job which is on a better shift, or in the next higher labor grade, or is pleasanter in some other respect."[11] If even this small ambition is frustrated, they try to better their position on their present job by getting the newest and best machine, or a better work location. Or they may try to gain more money for the same job, for to many workers "more money is virtually the whole meaning of occupational progress."[12] When asked if they had had promotions, a frequent response reported by Reynolds was, "Oh yes, I've had three raises since I came with the company." These findings were confirmed by Dofny and David, who found that workers in three Montreal plants expected only minimal promotions and considered that an increase in salary would be an improvement of their position.[13] With such modest ambitions, it is not difficult in an affluent economy to have a "sense of mobility."

Special notice should be taken at this point of the situation of the lower level white collar worker whose status has fallen as a result of the same technical, economic, and social changes that produced a rise in status for the blue collar worker. This group has always identified with the middle class, and this identification was, and is, very important to it. There is evidence that many white collar workers may try to cling to distinctions in terms of pay or promotion which make no sense in terms of distributive justice, since their qualifications, skills, and training differ less and less from those of blue collar workers. These demands to maintain traditional distinctions that are no longer functional may become an issue of considerable importance, since they are certain to arouse resentment among blue collar workers. Sturmthal mentions that one of the longest strikes in German postwar history originated in an issue of this kind.[14]

Geographic Mobility

There seems to be plenty of evidence of geographic mobility. People in the American economy, using this as the prototype of the mass consumption society, hold many different jobs, especially during their first ten years of employment; they often change residence, employer, and even occupation or industry. Palmer's study of six major U.S. cities shows that between 1940 and 1949 the mean number of jobs held per worker was 2.7, and the change of jobs often involved the change of employers one or two times. One-third of the workers sampled had moved their place of residence during that time. There is an even greater rate of mobility among *young* men, those between twenty-five and thirty-four years of age having an average of 3.4 jobs, and 50 per cent of these changes involve change of employer, industry, and occupation.[15] Palmer found that the difference in mobility rates among young workers resulted from their greater concern both for wages and for the intrinsic interest of the work. After the age of thirty-five, not only does a worker lose interest in changing employment, but his aspirations change and are modified, so that he is primarily interested in job security.[16]

These findings prove true in general for Canada also. A DBS study showed that 57.3 per cent of single men in 1957–58 changed jobs, as compared to 49 per cent of married men—a high rate in either case.[17] Peitchinis also comments that: "As one might expect, the older the worker gets the less mobile he tends to become . . . during the period 1956–60 an average of 38 per cent of persons 65 years of age and over changed jobs, compared with 66 per cent of young men under 20 years of age."[18]

Technical Mobility

Technical mobility, or the willingness and capacity to adapt to technological change, will be discussed in considerable detail in chapter 7 (Organizational Relationships). Here we will discuss only those general conditions which contribute to technical mobility. It may, and often does, involve geographical and/or occupational mobility, and differs from the other two in that it is usually less voluntary. Technological change is usually imposed on workers from outside, and the incidence of technical mobility among workers is therefore not so much a product of desire for it as of the general level of technology in the environment to which they are exposed. A worker's mobility in this case is therefore measured in terms of his speed of relearning and his acceptance of the principle of change.

The same factors which predispose people to accept occupational and geographical mobility, or for that matter any other kind of change, seem to apply in the case of technical mobility. A young, unmarried man of few years on a particular job is likely to accept change much more readily than women, older, married men, or people with longer attachment to an occupation or a job.[19] There is evidence that a high general level of education makes technical change more acceptable, whereas skills acquired only through long experience, such as fishing, mining, or highly skilled trades hinder a man's willingness to change. Other factors important in determining a worker's adaptation to technical change are the degree to which previous work roles were integrated with community values, the extent of previous experience with modern methods or equipment, the personal gains or losses the worker expects from technical change, and finally, the extent to which he is consulted and informed of changes which are about to occur in his work.

These points are best illustrated by contrasting a "modern" community with a more traditional one facing change. In small fishing or mining communities, everyone knows everyone else, work is the centre of life, and a man's identity in the community is directly related to his work. Change of method or industry in such a situation threatens not only a man's hard-acquired skills, but all his social relations, and often his cultural values as well. He will probably not have experienced many changes in production methods in his lifetime, nor will he be used to thinking in terms of highly mechanized or rationalized operations. A man who is faced with technical change in such a community and in such a situation will anticipate only loss of all those things that have had meaning to him, and is not likely to expect any gains. He will probably resist the change and remain technically nonmobile.

On the other hand, in a larger or more diversified community, change is more often experienced; the unity between working life and social life no longer exists, and it is easier to change employment. An OECD study found, also, that rural workers who had had some experience with modern agricultural machinery and methods adapted more easily to industrial work than those who had not.[20] Pécaut believes that where change constitutes a reality of everyday experience, technical change is seen as having positive economic meaning, and perhaps even social meaning to the individual, and these expectations lead to a positive attitude toward it. "Where community consciousness makes a change in behaviour less likely to occur, this is because it produces expectations which are limited to the existing social situation. Acceptance of change implies the creation of new expectations."[21] As we mentioned earlier, participation in modern consumption values is an experience in constant change which also creates expectation of personal gain to be obtained from technical change and predisposes people to accept it.

On the other hand, even workers in modern factories, especially if they are skilled and the change involves downgrading or obsolescence of these skills, will resist the change. Like the fisherman or the miner, workers see their social positions, at least in the factory community, threatened, and their expectations of gains from the new technology are low. As we stated in the discussion of technological change, these fears may or may not be well grounded. Some workers may, indeed, stand only to lose through technical change, but others may be little affected or may stand to gain, through retraining and general rise in productivity or job enlargement. The resistance to change by those adversely affected by it is justified and reasonable, but often such reluctance seems to be little more than fear of the unknown, a preference for the known evil. People will sometimes stay at near-starvation levels, rather than eat unaccustomed foods, for example. Whatever the case may prove to be, workers are better able to respond positively and realistically to the prospect of becoming technically mobile when they have been consulted and included in management plans from the beginning,[22] and the consultation process may also help to remind management of the very real human problems which often accompany change and which require some immediate solutions.

Geographic and technical mobility, when they operate well, are both important means of allowing supply and demand to smooth out disparities in wage levels and opportunity structure which occur in every national economy, and which are accentuated by technological change. Thus, if the city offers better opportunities and higher wages, labour moves from rural areas to the city; if British Columbia can offer more, workers are attracted from the Maritime Provinces or other depressed areas; if a factory can offer higher wages because of more efficient methods, that factory will draw the workers it needs from less efficient industries; and within a given plant, workers will be willing to learn new techniques and use new machines because they believe that they will have higher wages or better opportunities as a result. The system does not work perfectly, but it helps.

The Sense of Mobility

That the existence of all three kinds of mobility possibilities produces confidence and optimistic expectations is well documented by U.S. studies. The Palmer study reported that when people change jobs voluntarily, more than half of them think they are getting ahead.[23] *Fortune* magazine found in 1940 (not a year particularly good for optimism, since the depression was just ending and the United States was not yet in the war, so that the economy was not booming) that in a national survey 56.3 per cent of the sample felt that "the years ahead hold for [them] personally a good chance for advancement."[24] Katona cites similar expectations based on surveys of consumer finances conducted by the Michigan Survey Research Center in 1954 and 1962.[25] A breakdown by age and income of these responses shows definitely the greater optimism and expectations of the young, particularly in the higher income groups.

This "sense of mobility opportunities" is bolstered by the existence of other factors in the American situation:

(1) a philosophy of equalitarianism generally accepted in the U.S. and supported by the emphasis on making education available to all so that everyone may have, insofar as possible, the same chance of success.

(2) the absence of a feudal past [with its legitimation of hereditary social class].

(3) the pattern of business careers at the bottom [small private entrepreneurs, usually from the manual worker group] and at the top which seem to reflect and support the same belief in equality of opportunity.

(4) the combination of relative wealth and mass produced consumer goods which, as we have said so often, has had the effect of minimizing the differences between the standard of living of the working class and the middle class.[26]

The American social structure has been referred to by Parsons as a

relatively loose one characterized by a certain vagueness.[27] This loose-
ness reduces the strain in cases where there is a discrepancy between income and occupational status; for example, when a son makes more
money or is in an occupation of higher prestige than is his father, or
when a leading scientist makes less than does a corporation lawyer. These
people do not have to compare themselves directly with each other.
Equally important is the fact that such indefiniteness makes possible the
belief that opportunities are open to all. It gives a "sense of mobility,"
even if not actually experienced, and an accompanying optimism so important to a mass consumption economy and a democratic society.

Blocks to the Sense of Mobility

Although the "sense of mobility" is highly prevalent in the American
society, it is not so evident in Canada and Western Europe, where occupational, geographical, and technical mobility opportunities are not so
widespread as in the United States. Let us first consider occupational
mobility.

Lipset, in a study of the value structures of four English-speaking
democracies, shows that in those values and qualities of mind now
widely accepted as being functional to a technologically advanced
society, the United States is first, Australia second, Canada third, and
Great Britain last.[28] As Kaspar Naegele has expressed it: "there is less
emphasis in Canada on equality than there is in the United States. . . .
In Canada there seems to be a greater acceptance of limitation, of
hierarchical patterns. There seems to be less optimism, less faith in the
future, less willingness to risk capital or reputation. In contrast to America, Canada is a country of greater caution, reserve, and restraint."[29]

Lipset argues that Canada does not encourage achievement as much
as the United States or Australia by pointing out that Canada had (in
the 1940s) less than one-third the United States' student proportion in
colleges and universities, twice that of the English, but—amazingly—
less than the Filipinos or Puerto Ricans.[30] As Porter says, "Collective
goals do not seem to have been defined, however vaguely, in terms of
increasing opportunities through free universal education."[31] He demonstrates this point by comparing the situation in Quebec which, until very
recently, had the poorest record for providing public education of any
province. In 1931, for example, there were more immigrant males in
Quebec in the professions and clerical occupations than there were of
those born in Canada, although the opposite was the case in all other

provinces.[32] This situation, as we pointed out in the discussion on education, is changing rapidly now, but it illustrates the nature and recentness of the change.

This mobility deprivation exists not only in French Canada but in the rest of Canada as well. The Department of Labour studied five skilled occupations typical of high level industrialization: tool and die makers, sheet metal workers, draughtsmen, electronic technicians, and floor moulders. Eight hundred randomly selected people were interviewed. About 35 per cent of all those interviewed received most of their training outside Canada. The survey concluded that "training facilities in Canada were failing to keep pace with manpower requirements, and this was particularly pronounced in the more highly skilled occupations."[33] Furthermore, the level of education required for these jobs was going up, and the report showed that those with the higher levels of general education were more likely to be selected for formal training (apprenticeship) within the industry.[34] Once again, those with educational tools tend to accumulate advantages and widen the mobility gap between themselves and those without adequate education or training.

In recent years, Canadian immigration policy has tended to encourage the immigration of skilled labour and even of professionals, so that in 1955 immigrants accounted for about one-quarter of all professional workers in Canada. In the same period, 35.6 per cent of immigrant workers were in this category, or that of skilled labour, as compared to 22.5 per cent of the total Canadian labour force.[35] Closing off these avenues of upward mobility to the native population by importing better-trained people from elsewhere could have the effect of making Canadian workers feel that opportunities are limited in Canada. Porter feels that this policy of encouraging the immigration of skilled and professional manpower has had the even more important effect of making it unnecessary, or at least of relieving the pressure, to reform and renovate Canadian education in such a way as to offer the native-born worker better training and more opportunities. "Where Canadian immigration policy seeks skilled and professional workers as an alternative to educational reforms, mobility deprivation for Canadians continues."[36]

Mobility opportunities are even less in Britain. Miller's index of "inequality of opportunity" showed this factor to be highest in Britain and, conversely, that an index of "equality of opportunity" showed this factor to be lower in Britain than in any of eighteen countries for which data were available.[37] This is not surprising. Britain is poorer, has an older, more rigid class structure, and no "frontier" of escape within the country; that is, there is little opportunity for people to break out of their situation by changing occupations or by getting more education. Alford suggests that Australia also shows strong symptoms of lack of mobility opportunity as a result of inadequate educational opportunities and "frontiers." The same conditions exist in many Western European countries.

The effects of the status loss of white collar workers are uncertain. Lipset and Bendix state that "the downward mobile . . . behave similarly in all countries: they vote more conservatively than the stationery members of the class into which they have fallen."[38] On the other hand, Alford and Miller suggest that the high rate of downward mobility in Great Britain among nonmanual workers (42 per cent of the sons of nonmanual fathers are in manual positions in Britain, as compared to only 25 per cent in the United States) may reinforce the voting along class lines which is found in that country. They felt that white collar workers, always identifying with the middle class, might react negatively to the experience of loss of status by voting Left.[39] These studies, however, dealt with people who had jobs of lower prestige than those with which they started or than those held by their fathers. In the case of clerical workers who have not changed their occupation, but whose occupation itself has lost status, we suggest that voting or other political behaviour may depend on how workers define their new situation. As we have seen, those white collar workers who consider themselves as part of the working class tend to vote Labour or Democratic, while those who cling to their identification with the middle class can be expected to vote Conservative or Republican. If our hypothesis is correct, a study to determine what proportion of clerical workers in automated offices are making each kind of choice would be valuable in predicting both voting and union affiliation.

The results of Lipset's study of value structures show that the greater élitism and lower equalitarianism are partly the cause of what Lipset sees as greater respect for law in Canada and Britain. The fact that there are fewer and less powerful extremist movements, such as McCarthyism or that of the Ku Klux Klan, in Canada and in Britain is also evidence of élitism, "reflecting the ability of a more unified and powerful élite to control the system."[40] Finally, he found interesting differences in values shown in the reactions to the demands of military life by the four English-speaking groups during World War II.

The British and, to a lesser degree, the Canadians accepted the need to conform to the rigid hierarchical structure of the military; while

Australians and Americans showed deep resentment at having to exhibit deference to superiors. I have been told by nationals of different countries that in London bars during both world wars Americans and Australians tended to associate with each other, while Canadians were more likely than the Australians to prefer British companions to Americans.[41]

The reason for belabouring here what may seem obvious is that these traditionalist, élitist, ascriptive (a person is valued for *who* he is, not what he *does*) elements in Canadian and British society tend to lower the "sense of mobility." Finally, it is at least a plausible argument that in countries where mobility opportunities are *felt* to be low, there is a greater tendency for workers to try to improve their lot by changing the whole social system through political action. Daniel Bell has called this ideological or social movement unionism, as opposed to market-unionism which is concerned simply with the conditions under which men sell their labour. The appearance of leftist labour parties in such European countries as Italy and France may be examples of this social movement unionism, as is the existence of a strong Labour party in Britain. In Canada, the support given by the CCL to the CCF and the CLC to the NDP indicates a tendency for unions to adopt ideological unionism to a greater extent than unions in the United States have done,[42] a difference which is congruent with the disparity in mobility possibilities in the two countries, if the thesis is correct.

This tendency for labour to try to improve its position through reform of the social and economic system was most marked during the thirties when the United States lowered its immigration quotas drastically, thus reducing still further the mobility opportunities of Canadian workers. In French Canada, where the mobility chances for the French-speaking workers are even less than for the rest of Canada, the emphasis on ideological unionism is unequivocal. Jean Marchand commented on this when he was president of the Confederation of National Trade Unions.

Modern trade-unionism aims at protecting the workers not only in the factory or at the office, but wherever their interests are at stake. Thus it is concerned with legislation, education, economic orientation, social security and even political problems. In the pursuit of its objectives, it will inevitably refer to an ideology, or a set of ideologies, and express its own conception of the enterprise, the State, social security, economic activity and mankind. From the moment it turns to these questions, it enters a world of diversity where opinions, convictions, beliefs are extremely at variance. Trying to crush these tendencies under artificially unified structures, on the pretense that more power and efficiency would be obtained, can only result in impoverished ideologies, social paralysis and a decline in the vitality of the labour movement.[43]

We cannot say with certainty to what extent this relative lack of occupational and social mobility in the Canadian economy affects the average Canadian's aspirations and expectations. It can be argued that lack of this kind of mobility is not felt keenly because the Canadian worker can always go to the United States if opportunities are not sufficient at home. He can and often does do this, as indicated by the continual concern in Canada over the extent of emigration to the United States. On the other hand, the one survey of Canadian mobility attitudes of which we are aware, the Dofny-David (see p. 64), is again offered, this time to show that workers do feel the lack of occupational mobility. One of the favourite mobility dreams of American manual workers is that of starting a little business of their own. The existence of this possibility has been cited as one of the important sources of the "sense of mobility." Lipset and Bendix, in their study of the Oakland, California area found that 66.7 per cent of manual workers had thought of doing this and that 41.5 per cent had actually tried it at some time during their working lives.[44] In Montreal, the number of workers who had *dreamed* of a business of their own was very similar—52.1 per cent; the number who had actually *tried* it was sharply different—only 5.8 per cent. The comparison suggests a marked difference between American and Canadian workers in optimism or belief in the possibility of mobility, at least by the means of owning a little business.[45]

We have also seen that there is not as much geographical and technical mobility in Canada as in the United States. Greater physical and cultural distances between provinces and lower educational and income levels might be responsible for some of this difference. Moreover, to the degree that management is élitist rather than equalitarian and stands on management rights rather than accepting the principle that, in the interest of all concerned, the worker should be informed in advance about technical change, technical mobility may be more difficult than it need be. In any case, the fact seems to be that inadequate mobility opportunities can be expected to be the cause of much discontent among workers, reflected in what may seem unreasonable demands on unions by members and on management by unions. If the only way a man can achieve success is through getting more money (whether through wages or fringe benefits), then workers' demands for money are going to be exorbitant indeed.

Implications of Labour Mobility in a Mass Consumption Society

The society that offers opportunities to develop aspirations (as is implied by mass educational systems being introduced in all advanced countries) should also make serious efforts to offer labour mobility opportunities. Our study has suggested that there exist in Canada and Britain some serious disjunctures in this regard. Such disjunctures exist even in the United States, particularly with regard to the Black population. We can expect that workers so trapped will feel discouraged about promotion possibilities, and about achieving recognition and responsibility through their own efforts. Some people will react to this situation by losing interest, others by leaving to find better opportunities elsewhere. These are often the workers most able to compete and to get good jobs abroad. Their leaving might be expected, in turn, to reduce the level of productivity of the remaining work force, as demonstrated in depressed areas such as the Maritimes or Southern United States. This in turn imposes limits on wage levels and leads to more dissatisfaction among remaining workers. Finally, there are those who will try to change things, be it within unions, through collective bargaining, or through political action, in such a way as to get better opportunities for themselves. If the disparity between aspirations encouraged and opportunities offered is great enough, as in the case of the American Blacks, the situation becomes explosive.

There are many who decry the materialism and the greed represented by a continual accumulation of goods, and the waste involved in disposing of them. They also fear the destruction of spiritual values and point to the tastelessness of much of the consumption and of the leisure activities indulged in by the mass of consumers. Much of this is well founded. But we should perhaps remind ourselves that these complaints seem always to have been voiced by older, privileged groups confronted by new groups learning to use the same privileges. Voltaire said, "History is the sound of silver slippers descending the stairs and the clump of hob-nailed boots ascending." He had the misfortune to anticipate the French Revolution. In the mass consumption society, he might have witnessed the ascending of hob-nailed boots without any descending of silver slippers. As Fourastié says: "A man who two centuries ago would not even have learned to read, if he had survived to maturity, profits by his windows, the central heating of his apartment, and the 300,000 copies of the newspaper for which he writes, to announce that humanity has arrived at the last stage of barbarism."[46]

Foote and Hatt maintain that a mass consumption economy depends on a "massification" of taste, and that only to the extent that the customer will accept standardization can a particular article be produced at a price that all can afford—"because it is beneath the dignity of no one to eat Campbell's soup, everyone can afford it." The authors emphasize the relationship between economic advancement and social equality. "Social demand for greater equality may thus lead to economic demand which may in turn make it possible to develop the productivity which makes possible the degree of equality . . . that perhaps only an advanced society can afford. Thus in judging social values we may as a society be on the verge of discovering that *general economic advancement and social equalitarianism are interdependent* while retention of steep stratification and rivalrous *personal* mobility is economically stultifying."[47]

This hypothesis, taken together with the levelling of hierarchies within automated industries and the general social tendencies toward equalitarianism, suggests that occupational mobility of the individual may be of much less importance in the future than it has been in the past. As we have seen, where wages are high and work is meaningless, men will seek status, creativity, and success symbols outside work. As we stated before, we do not believe this is more than a temporary acceptance of an unsatisfactory situation; but while it exists and where wages are not high enough to offer consumption possibilities as compensation for meaningless work, the ambitions of workers will still seek expression in demands for promotion opportunities on the job or pressure for higher wages, or, perhaps, in changes in the social order itself.

6

Changing Life Styles

We will now consider to what degree the changing environmental experiences have altered the attitudes and life style of the emerging worker.

Blue collar workers have not only experienced the most dramatic change in life styles of any group in the society, but also have represented for some time the majority of organized union members. On the other hand, the white collar occupations are growing rapidly and may, in the future, employ a majority of the workers in the economy. Because the lower echelons of this group are joining unions and are in other respects becoming more and more like blue collar workers, we will include them in our exploration.

There are three major divisions among manual workers which derive from their training, status, and the kind of work they do: the skilled, the semiskilled, and the unskilled. These divisions are important enough to produce different attitudes, different life experiences and life styles.

We have chosen to concentrate our analysis on the semiskilled worker rather than the skilled or the unskilled worker for several reasons. The other two groups have experienced less change than has the semiskilled group since the rise in the standard of living after World War II. The skilled worker, because he is too well trained in a specialty, is often less able and less willing to learn new methods than the semiskilled worker who has less at stake in the old system. As a result, he is often bypassed in the automated factory, and semiskilled workers promoted to better positions. Also, there is evidence that because of their control of the apprenticeship possibilities, skilled workers have tended to keep the trade in the family. The result has been that, since it is difficult to get into the trades, semiskilled workers on their way up tend to bypass the skilled workers and become nonmanual workers, and that people who are downwardly mobile tend to fall from white collar to semiskilled positions. "The skilled, with status satisfaction, relative job security, and traditional style of life, have little incentive to 'try out' for another set of life goals."[1]

The unskilled worker, on the other hand, is one who somehow has been denied the opportunities to participate in the mainstream of the economy and, lacking in training or in general education, he finds himself unable to get ahead. He may be a Negro, an Eskimo, or an Indian, or he may have had the bad luck to be born in a Newfoundland fishing village, a Nova Scotia or West Virginia mining town, or the slums of London. The proportion of unskilled labourers in the labour force is diminishing, but for those who remain, life is marked by poverty and frequent unemployment. It has changed very little because of affluence.

For these reasons, it is on the semiskilled industrial workers and what we might call the semiskilled office workers that we want to focus our attention. These two groups will be further classified as either "modern" or "traditional." A modern worker has at least a high-school education, a relatively high income, and works in an automated or semiautomated plant. His work experience is the most advanced in terms of technological change. While this is a model, not a definition, of the modern worker, we think we can assume, based on experience in the United States, that this kind of worker may represent the majority in the near future in Canada and Western Europe, as he does now in the United States. The traditional worker has little education, a lower income, and less experience with technical change. We do not necessarily imply a time element; he exists in the present as well as the past and is defined by his social, educational, and work experience, rather than by his age or time.

The life of a man can be divided roughly into three principal sectors: family and personal life, work life, and community life. In these ways, then, we will contrast the lives of traditional workers with those of modern workers.

Community Relationships

Since the beginning of the Industrial Revolution, workers have been moving from rural to urban areas where industrial jobs were to be found.

The modern industrial city was built on this basis, and, even now, cities have working-class residential districts clustered around industrial areas. Whether near the centre of the city or on its periphery, such housing is definitely urban, consisting of flats and some older houses, crowded, and often in the first stages of deterioration. More prosperous middle-class residents, as ecologists such as Burgess have shown us, moved in successive waves to the newer, less crowded neighbourhoods and finally, as the city continued to grow, to suburbs just outide the city.

Worker affluence has begun to change this pattern. Dobriner in *Class in Suburbia* makes it clear that in the United States and Britain the move of the working classes to the suburbs from older city neighbourhoods is a growing trend, newer in the United States than in Britain, presumably because urbanization is a newer phenomenon in the United States.[2] The move to suburbia seems to occur only after population density has reached certain levels. Clark suggests that in the new working-class suburbs of Toronto, which grew up in the 1950s, it was the young people of under thirty-five years with incomes ranging from $3,000 to $7,200 who moved out of the older working-class neighbourhoods in the city in search of housing. The majority of these people living in less expensive suburbs such as Richmond Acres or Lyons had not previously owned their own houses, and had been unable to find housing in the city. The move then represented an effort not only to find any kind of housing, but also to improve their housing, and was possible only for those working-class families whose incomes had reached a level making home-ownership possible.[3]

The traditional, urban blue collar worker lives in flats or apartments near the centre of the city, in a neighbourhood, usually, of workers like himself. Often he lives within walking distance of parents, brothers and sisters, and other relatives. He probably belongs to a union and his wife might attend church, but their affiliation with other community organizations is practically nil. The husband spends his free time drinking in pubs or playing cards with the boys. The wife spends her free time with relatives and often does not even accompany her husband on holidays, which often consist of fishing or hunting trips. In general, hardship and adversity, frequently experienced, produce withdrawal symptoms and a sense of helplessness rather than determined efforts to cope; as Chinoy found among automobile workers, "only if at first you *do* succeed do you try again."[4] If sickness or unemployment strikes, the extended family closes ranks and cares for its members, insofar as possible. W. F. Whyte tells a story illustrating the dependency of the old-style worker on his family network, rather than on community organizations and services.

During the depression four children were born to the Elnos. They had to flee to steadily smaller and poorer apartments, and the children were reduced to half-starvation rations, which kept them sorely undernourished and chronically ill. Unemployment and their hopelessly large family wore away the determination and the morale of the parents, especially of Jim. They separated twice, and Jim deserted once but returned. He was arrested two or three times for panhandling while drunk. He beat his wife several times, when he was drunk. . . .

But Pearl still had her own parental family. Her father and mother, and her sisters, together with their husbands, formed a closely organized and loyal clan, which repeatedly rescued her and her seven children. The sisters took them in, when Jim was violently drunk, or when they were evicted for inability to pay the rent. They bought the children clothes, and helped feed them. Pearl's mother, still able to hold a job at sixty, borrowed money on her home to lend to Jim, when he was employed by the Works Progress Administration. She came up from southern Indiana repeatedly to care for the children, so that Pearl could work as a waitress, and as a machine operator, to help feed the children while Jim was unemployed. One of Pearl's sisters opened a tavern recently and employed the mother, who in turn helped Pearl's family.[5]

That this traditional pattern of dependence on the extended family exists in Canadian cities has been documented, at least in part, by Pineo in Hamilton and by Garigue in Montreal.[6]

The modern, blue collar worker lives in a working-class suburb, where he probably owns his own house. The Kraft report recently discovered that nearly 75 per cent of all union members in the United States under forty years old now live in suburbs, a figure that gives some idea of the strength and speed of the change in this part of workers' life style. Owning his own house gives the worker a great sense of having moved up in the world. Berger interviewed men who had been moved from city flats to a new suburb by the Ford Company. Their reactions to the move are reflected in such statements as: "I'm sure glad the plant forced us to move: if it hadn't we'd probably still be in housing (government flats); it was just too cheap to leave."[7] Chinoy found that automobile workers in Detroit regarded the owning of houses as an important index of mobility. A welder living in the slums believed that, "We're all working for one purpose, to get ahead. I don't think a person should be satisfied. My next step is a nice little modern house of my own. That's what I mean by bettering yourself—or getting ahead."[8] British workers were even more enthusiastic about their move from council houses to houses of their own. As one worker said: "Everybody should have a house of his own, something to work for."[9]

The move to the suburbs also changes the pattern of social relationships. Zweig found that people on the new estates in England "are more house-proud, but less gregarious. You can walk for a mile or two before you see anybody on the estates."[10] Since there are no pubs in the new suburbs, husbands tend to stay home in the evenings, working in the garden, fixing up the house, watching TV. Two American workers express their attitude: "Before I was married I used to spend time with a bunch of friends making all the bars. Was out raising hell a lot. Now I bring my beer home"[11] and "I'm a homebody. We don't go out much. I chew the rag with my wife, or someone stops in. Like last night. The friend that lives across the street, the tinsmith, was here . . . we had a beer. Not that the beer was important. Just something to talk on."[12] Berger found that visiting with friends and neighbours increased with the move to the suburbs, but not much. There was still a tendency either to visit with relatives, if there were any available, or for the family to keep to itself.

Clark was able to confirm much of this description of modern working-class suburban living. He concluded that the majority of suburbanites around Toronto were under forty years, Canadian born, Protestant, of British origin, and earning incomes between three thousand and ten thousand dollars a year. Their occupations were those of unskilled, semi-skilled, and skilled workers, white collar employees, and small business-men. Only two of the fifteen suburbs studied were of the upper middle-class, planned community type described in *Crestwood Heights*, a study of a Toronto suburb. Clark's investigation can be compared with Berger's study of a working-class suburb in the United States, or Zweig's study in Britain, and the findings are very similar. He finds that Toronto workers are proud of their houses, would not leave the suburb even though buying the house is often a financial burden, that they do not join community organizations, at least not for quite a while, and they entertain very little. They are "privatized" or family-centred. Clark, however, believes that this lack of sociability is caused less by innate working-class attitudes than by the fact that, with young children and debts, neither husband nor wife has the time, energy, or money to participate. One wife told him: "It is difficult right now—you see people are just getting settled. They cannot be interested in organizations. Added to that there is the problem of baby-sitters. We can't get any around here. None of my friends is interested in organizations. They can't go out as they, too, have small children. We do not even go to movies. We sit and watch TV. Husbands are tired too. . . . Most of us here have to work hard in the house. We are poor. . . ."[13]

Another wife illustrated her busy schedule: "I look after my neighbour's children while she works from 7:45 a.m. to 6:00 p.m. And then I go home and get meals and look after my own place—there's no time left over. My husband doesn't belong to any organizations either. He works shifts. We're both too tied up. I didn't belong to any organizations before we came up here. I worked there too."[14]

There is one important influence tending to change the pattern of informal relationships of the modern blue collar worker. The wife who is home most of the day begins, after a time, to participate in such middle-class activities as kaffeeklatsching, going to Parent-Teacher Association meetings, and consulting teachers, doctors, and dentists about the children; or, if she works, she is likely to have a white collar job and meet middle-class people. In either case, wives exert a certain pressure on the family to adopt new sociability patterns and new values. The men spend almost their entire time with other blue collar workers in the plant, and their social life or organizational life, if any, will be with the same kinds of persons that they are. The wife, on the other hand, especially if she works, or if she lives in a normally mixed suburban community, has a wider range of contact with nonmanual workers or their wives. Husbands in Berger's working-class suburb seemed to display a certain indignation about their wives' participation in these kaffeeklatsches because "it isn't the kind of thing factory workers' wives usually do." Berger comments, "The ability of the wives to be sociable is without doubt related to the fact that on the whole they are considerably better educated than their husbands." In this study 26 per cent of the men and 40 per cent of the women revealed a high school education or better.[15] Hurvitz noted that "the wife is more likely to develop middle-class values and attitudes faster than her husband."[16] Berger found that *Parents* magazine was the authority on child rearing most frequently consulted by wives of auto workers, although the books of Dr. Spock were read as well. Both of these introduce wives to child-rearing practices not previously known in working-class families.

Buying a house in the suburbs, then, changes the social setting of the modern working-class family and brings it into the general standard consumption pattern and consumer financial arrangements such as mortgages, credit, and insurance typical of the mass consumption economy. The family buys a refrigerator, washing machine, vacuum cleaner, and TV to go in their new house. A car becomes essential for commuting. To finance this, the modern young worker is more likely to use credit. His wife, especially if there are no children, is more likely to work than is the case with the traditional working-class family. In this new setting there is less chance of depending on an extended family for support or sociability, so that the family becomes more "privatized," spending most of their time together. There are, at the same time, discernible pressures to adopt new social patterns and values, involving closer relationships with friends and neighbours and middle-class ideas of "keeping up appearances." Examples of this are the comments of British workers concerning the way in which the family used the house: "In the previous house the front door was never meant to be used; we had a settee across it. Everyone, including the post-man, called at the back door. Now it is different. We've moved to the front" and "In the other house the front room was never used except for Christmas. If I lit a fire in the front room we always seemed to get back into the kitchen. I suppose we were used to it. Now it's different."[17]

All these tendencies are further reinforced by the new leisure patterns of the working class which reflect both affluence and the emphasis on the nuclear family. This centring on the immediate family is both a necessary condition for job mobility, particularly geographical and occupational, and is a change which mobility brings about. As we have shown earlier, the same leisure pursuits can, and often are, followed by all social classes, and workers are aware that this and other forms of consumption have reduced the differences between classes. It is one of their strongest motivations for acquiring the standard package of consumer goods.

On the other hand, the modern worker does not join community organizations any more frequently than the traditional one does, and his union allegiance seems by most accounts to be considerably lessened. Perhaps of even greater concern is the level of alienation among workers who do belong to unions. One study estimated that the average attendance at union meetings is between 2 per cent and 6 per cent of the membership.[18] There may be many reasons for this, some of which are discussed in other parts of this study, but it is generally believed that traditional militant unionism was a product of strong class consciousness. The modern worker certainly has less of this than the traditional worker had. For example, British workers told Zweig: "Classes are coming nearer—the top grades of the working class are middle class really." "There are no differences: I live in the same neighbourhood as my manager, have the same kind of house and have a car." "Actually I don't see any difference: I earn as much as a shopkeeper."[19]

It is interesting to note, on the other hand, that all studies have shown that affluence and/or the move to the suburbs have not changed the way workers vote. In the United States, workers have traditionally voted Democratic, and the Kraft poll taken in January, 1967 showed that 58 per cent identify themselves as Democrats, 16 per cent as Republicans, 17 per cent as independents, and 9 per cent as not sure. These results pertain to workers of whom 78 per cent make $5,000 to $15,000 per year (family income), and 46 per cent are in the $7,500 to $15,000 range. Fifty per cent of all union members in the United States now live in suburbs. In spite of this, the proportion of those who would vote Democratic has not changed appreciably since 1964 when these same workers polled voted 60 per cent for Johnson and 12 per cent for Goldwater.[20] Berger found, similarly, that the move to the suburbs had no effect on the voting patterns of automobile workers.[21] In Britain, Goldthorpe and his associates found that, "our affluent workers have been quite stable in their support of Labour: 69 per cent have been regular Labour voters from 1945 onwards, or from whenever they first voted, as opposed to 12 per cent being regular Conservative supporters."[22]

The main exception to this was found among workers who had white collar affiliations through wives who either came from the white collar class or had worked in a white collar job, or through fathers who had nonmanual occupations. Goldthorpe found that white collar affiliations were the single most important influence in lowering Labour voting among manual workers, when it occurred.[23] White collar identification with the middle class can be expected, then, to act as another force blurring status gaps and producing attitude homogenization in the lower levels of the work hierarchy. It may also, as the white collar group grows in numbers, lead to greater political conservatism at the polls, unless, of course, this tendency is offset by other white collar workers who, as a result of technological change in their jobs, begin to identify with the working class. Our guess (and in the absence of studies of the problem it is only that) is that in the United States and Canada, where social class lines are not rigid and where educational levels are high, the "pull" is likely to be up rather than down; that is, more working-class people will begin to identify with the middle class, rather than white collar people adopting the attitudes and voting behaviour of blue collar workers. If this occurs, then conservatism should increase.

To summarize, we may say that house owning in the suburbs, higher educational levels, affluence, mobility, and contact with mass consumption and mass leisure values have eroded the class consciousness of the modern worker considerably. This may effect his union allegiance, but it has not yet affected voting behaviour nor his low level of interest in community organizations, unless he has white collar affiliations. These influences, however, have lessened extended family ties and strengthened those of the nuclear family, a circumstance that may be expected eventually to lead to greater dependency on and interest in community services.

Family Relationships

The changes which have occurred in family relationships are striking. The traditional worker is authoritarian in his relationship to both wife and children and given to physical punishment for children and wife-beating when under the influence of stress and alcohol. Husbands rarely talk about their work, and often wives know only vaguely what their husbands do for a living. He spends his working and leisure life with other men of his own educational and economic background, and usually of the same neighbourhood. His wife spends her time entirely in "doing for others"; taking care of the children, washing, ironing, housekeeping, cooking, etc. She has no hobbies, no outside interests and "restricted to the house, more than one out of three have 'never learned to drive a car' and would be hard pressed to find recreational outlets away from home."[24] She sees her mother and other members of her or his family almost every day. She feels that the world is chaotic, that economic insecurity is a constant threat, if not a reality, and that she has no power to shape her life or external events. "She seems to lack the inner resources —the self-direction, the confidence, the assertiveness, the will—to move about freely in the larger world."[25]

A study called *Workingman's Wife* revealed through various psychological tests that the blue collar wife, especially of the traditional kind, is emotionally and financially totally dependent on her husband, whom she nonetheless sees as "insensitive and inconsiderate, sometimes teasing, sometimes accusing, sometimes vulgar, always potentially withholding affection." In their sexual relations, she often feels that he treats her as an "object for his own personal gratification without the kind of tenderness she so much wants."[26]

She is basically an unorganized person without enough education and self-confidence to understand and manipulate her environment. She tends to be antiunion because the union ignores her; her only contact with its activities occurs during and as a result of strikes which threaten her livelihood. "In strikes at J. I. Case, Ford of Canada and elsewhere, the disgruntled housewife, unmoved by union élan, uninformed about strike issues and without money to run her house, has sparked back-to-work movements."[27]

It is possible that the increased status and influence of the wife in the modern working-class family, combined with these antiunion attitudes where they have persisted, may be one factor in causing workers to be more alienated or rebellious toward their unions than they were in the past.

The self-deprecatory feelings of most traditional semiskilled workers, based on the low prestige of their jobs and on their frequent inability to care adequately for their families, particularly if the families are large, is a basic fact of life which influences all the family relationships. The wife and soon the children are aware that the father's job is not as successful as others and is responsible for some of the economic insecurity from which they suffer. His wife, who shares his self-deprecatory feelings, may work, if necessary. Both parents will encourage their children to get enough education so they can obtain better jobs than their fathers and will urge their daughters to marry someone with more education. It is not easy for parents to say to their children, "Don't be like us." A West Virginian miner expresses his wish that his children better themselves: "My boy, he wants to be a mechanic and he hopes they'll take him in the Army when he gets old enough. This girl of mine, she's thirteen going on fourteen, and she wants to be a teacher. They talk about this all the time and while they're talking I'm hoping. And every night I pray: They've got to get out of here."[28]

In general, parents feel that children have to be tough to survive, and the father will be a strict and often harsh disciplinarian. As a Negro adolescent in Detroit remarked: "He [the father] tells us what to do, and if we don't do it he kicks the hell out of us."[29]

In the traditional working-class family, the many children are an important cause of chronic economic difficulties. A miner in West Virginia has to ask his oldest son to leave school so he can afford to send the younger ones. "In school the kids have to buy books, they got to buy lunches or take them and they got to have clothes. . . . You know kid's shoes. You can get them for $4 a pair made out of stuff like cardboard and the first rainstorm they're gone. . . . Right now four of my kids in school need shoes so bad if they don't get them they can't go to school no more."[30]

A Negro worker, who in good times made $120 a week, said: "The main problem with us has been that while our income went up, our family got bigger, so big that my income just couldn't keep up with it."[31]

Medical care is almost nonexistent for the traditional worker's family. Dentists or doctors are sought only when pain or illness is acute, and even then they may have difficulty getting a doctor to come to them. Corresponding to the general sense of helplessness, of low self-esteem, of mistrust of the future, and of ignorance, which plagued workers before the age of affluence and which still plagues some groups in our society, is the lack of interest in preventive medicine, dental care, or even medical care, except in emergencies. Just as these people tend to let machines and houses run down rather than keep them in good condition, so they seem to regard the body as simply another object to be worn out, but not repaired. Perhaps even more important, with large families, there was never enough money for anything except necessities of the moment. Children suffered a great deal from this state of affairs. A Negro worker who left North Carolina to work in Norfolk, Virginia, as a sheet metal worker, has passed from traditional to modern experiences and attitudes in his own lifetime. He describes the change:

> From $27 a week to $54 sure looked good. And don't let anyone fool you. It wasn't just the country boy looking at a lot of cash. Things really were better. We lived in three big rooms in a place that had a nice yard. Don't forget we had all lived together in one room before. We had never had our own private beds. We had slept in a house where rain came through the roof and soaked the bedclothes, where lots of nights when it was cold we couldn't take our clothes off to sleep. Here I was, 24 years old, and I had my first private bed, my first steak, my first pork chops. We'd raised hogs at home but we always had to sell the chops for cash. The family ate the fat. Now we had meat every day. Corned beef hash. Chops. Hamburger. Steak. Milk. Orange juice. My kids were getting strong.
>
> Back home when a kid got sick, there were home remedies but not much else. Now these kids were healthy because they ate well and they were in a clean house and out of the weather and they saw a doctor who made sure they were growing right. Back home on the farm when a kid didn't eat right and missed vitamins he didn't grow right and he could never make it up. It is not a word of lie when I tell you that going from my father's farm in Zebulon to a city job in Norfolk was like going from darkness to light.[32]

In the modern worker's family, husbands and wives act more as a couple and, if they have friends, they are mutual friends. The husband, as we have seen, shares his leisure time with his wife. Within the family, the husband participates more in helping his wife and in rearing the children than does the traditional worker. Zweig found that, "There is little doubt that the image of the stern, bullying, dominating and self-assertive father or of the absent father who took no interest in the children, leaving them to the mother, is fast disappearing, and the new image of a benevolent, friendly and brotherly father is emerging." And fathers remarked, "My father had power over us: I can't boss them." "I never saw in my younger days a man pushing a pram; he would have been a laughing stock. Now you see a great many men pushing them proudly." "I am not bossy. I try to be friendly to the children."[33]

That the status of the wife of the modern worker has improved is shown by her husband's sharing of her life, and this is demonstrated even more clearly by the greater equality enjoyed by the modern worker and his wife and their greater mutuality in sexual relations. Zweig found that two-thirds of the women in his group of modern workers felt that they were the equals of their husbands in family matters, and one-third professed the superiority of the male sex. By and large, younger women asserted their equality more firmly than did the older women. They made such remarks as, "It is stupid, the idea of a master" and "He doesn't keep me, so he is not in a position to order me about"—remarks which hardly sound like those of the bewildered and insecure traditional working-class wife.[34] Rainwater and Handel, who studied the traditional wife, make a distinction between the sexual relationship between husband and wife of traditional and modern working-class families. They found that in 57 per cent of cases studied, where man and wife shared most of their daily life and interests, both spouses speak of sexual relations as highly gratifying to both of them, as compared to 11 per cent of couples in the traditional, highly segregated role relationships.[35]

Mirra Komarovsky found that the attitudes of blue collar workers toward shared leisure between husband and wife, or conversely, the husband's right to go out irrespective of his wife's feelings, is correlated with education in a rather striking way. Couples were asked to comment on a hypothetical situation in which a wife objected that two nights a week was too often for her husband to leave her alone with the children, and that she wanted more of his company. The wife's view in the case was upheld by 41 per cent of the high school graduates and only by 26 per cent of those of less than high school education. Conversely, the husband's right to do as he chose was defended by 57 per cent of the less educated, but by only 35 per cent of the high school graduates. Since the modern worker has a higher level of education than the traditional one, we should expect him to have the higher evaluation of the wife's feelings, and consequently, of her status in the family.[36]

Some of this improvement in the wife's status, and the accompanying improvement in husband-wife relationships, is certainly due to the fact that increasingly the wife goes out to work, not because she must (which often undermines the relationship between them), but to improve the family standard of living. On the other hand, the fact that she shares in family financial responsibilities leads also to certain strains in the blue collar family. As we have seen, she is more likely to get a white collar job than is her husband, and in other ways, such as her higher level of education and greater exposure to middle-class values, she may adopt standards and values which are different from her husband's and which will, perhaps, add to his feeling of inadequacy or, at least, make him uncomfortable.

This strain, when it exists, is most clearly seen in child-rearing patterns. It is expressed, on the wife's part, by such statements as: "But why does he always complain about the kids? Who is he to talk? He wasn't such a big success to tell me how to raise the kids. If they grew up his way, they'd end up in the shop like him."[37] In such a situation, the children are likely to prefer the more permissive mother, and the father who still clings to many of his old-fashioned ideas is "then left feeling superfluous in the family, despite his sincere efforts to help his children grow up in a way that he believes will enable them to compete in the harsh world he has come to know."[38]

In general, however, the modern working class couple, particularly if they are young and educated, are united in a desire to obtain the best for their children—to provide all the things they missed, or all the things they think the children are entitled to. The traditional and the modern working class family are alike in that they tend to transfer many of their own frustrated ambitions to their children. The modern family realizes even more clearly, however, that the way to a better, more secure life lies through education.

This cherishing of the individual child is a product of, first, the diminishing size of the blue collar family. Families of modern orientation and education tend to limit the number of children to three or four—another way in which the middle class and the working class, starting from different positions, are reaching a new consensus. The middle-class family, which used to limit itself to two children, now tends toward three or four.[39] Second, the moving away from kinship networks of the traditional family has turned the blue collar family in on itself for entertainment, for companionship, and for self-realization. Each child then becomes important in the social and psychological structure of the family; all the family members are more important to each other than they were in the traditional family. Third, general prosperity which has existed for a generation now, plus rising incomes and the general rise in prestige levels of the occupational structure, have provided hope for the future and the means to reach goals, previously only dreamed of, for the majority of workers. Children then become their investment in a dream of the future—"What I can't accomplish my children will be able to do."

Affluence and education have given parents reason to hope for an even better life for their children and to believe that, in providing them with comforts and advantages which they never had, or at least not to the same extent, these children will be spared the insecurity they knew and will learn how to make the most of their opportunities. On this point, there is little difference between the traditional and the modern worker, except that the latter will have higher aspirations for his children. He will want them to go to college and be professionals.

A logger in Quebec, who feels trapped by his lack of education in a job that will "burn him out" by the time he is thirty-five, even if he manages to support his family that long, comments: "La prison, vous savez, c'est pas pire qu'icitte. Qu'est-ce que j'aimerais, ça serait de frapper une petite 'job' qui me donnerait assez d'argent pour faire vivre ma famille de 7 enfants. J'voudrais leur donner une chance de s'éduquer. J'sus prêt à faire tous les sacrifices pour eux autres, parce que je veux pas que mes enfants aient autant de misère que moi. . . ."[40]*

The same sentiments were expressed by automobile assembly line workers: "I never had a chance, but I want my kids to go to college and do something better than factory work." "If he goes into the factory [instead of finishing high school] I'll beat the hell out of him—except if he just goes in for a visit or if he goes to engineering school or learns a trade first."[41]

These exact feelings are echoed in the remarks of a logger whose wife had recently written him that his son had quit school to take a job as a clerk: "Heureusement qu'il n'avait pas choisi le bois, parce que je serais allé le chercher par les cheveux et je l'aurais ramené à la maison. Jamais un de mes enfants connaîtra dans le bois ce que j'ai connu. J'en ai un deuxième aux études et celui-là je vais le garder aussi longtemps que je

*A rough translation: "Prison, you know, is not worse than this. What I would like would be to get a small job which would give me enough money to support my family of seven children. I would like to give them a chance to get an education. I'm ready to make any sacrifices for them, because I don't want my children to have as much misery as I have had."

le pourrai. Je suis un peu pauvre, mais tout le revenu que j'aurai je vais lui donner pour son instruction."[42]*

British workers in modern plants say: "It is the finest thing there is to give the children every advantage" and "I scrubbed and scraped to give my children every chance."[43]

American packinghouse workers express these reactions: "I come from a pretty large family of six boys and one girl, and things was pretty rough, you know. And we never had too much—we always had somethin' to eat and a clean place to live in. But as far as that, that was about as far as it went. Now I got two children now: I got a boy three and a half and I got a boy one and a half, and I try to do everything in the world for those kids. I give them anything they want. In fact, it costs me quite a bit of money. They cost me all I make." "I tell you what I'm doing. I buy war bonds. I have $2.50 a week taken out of my pay every week; I don't even miss it. It's for the kids' education. I got about—oh I guess I got 25 or 26 of those $25.00 bonds, and that money I won't touch. I'll have to be awful hard up before I'll touch it. That's for the kids' education. . . . I figure on the kids living like—like they should and not having to put up—I don't want 'em workin' in a packin'-house."[44]

Work Relationships

According to our definition, the young, educated, and affluent worker should also work in an automated or semiautomated plant, if he is to qualify as "modern." The reason for this is that there are differences in the experience of working in such a plant which tend to colour a man's view of work, of management, and of the society in which he lives. We have, in various parts of this study, gone into these changes in the work environment in some detail and tried to analyze them. Here we would like to let the worker speak for himself, to explain the feelings he has about his work, which he brings home, to union meetings, or to his political activities and interests.

The remarks quoted above concerning the blue collar worker's hopes that his son will not go into a plant or factory express, by implication,

*A rough translation: "Happily he didn't choose the woods, because I would have gone after him and brought him back to the house by the hair. Never will one of my children know what I have known in the woods. I have a second son at school and I am going to keep him there as long as I can. I am poor, but all the income that I have I am going to give him for his education."

the worker's dislike of his work and his feeling that it is of low status. His self-deprecatory feelings are always there—he cannot avoid being aware that his semiskilled job marks him as a failure. If, in addition, the conditions of the job are unpleasant (as they often are in mass assembly plants—by our definition one of the "traditional" kinds of work experience), then a man's work experience becomes largely one of frustration and deprivation. To go to work each morning is to face a daily beating of the ego. The family naturally feels this. A child, whose father expressed deep dissatisfaction with his job, said: "Daddy is cranky all of the time. He used to take us to the movies, but now he doesn't any more." His wife remarked: "He is very unhappy with his job and it naturally reflects in his attitudes and conversation at home. His naturally happy-go-lucky attitude is disappearing. The reasons he doesn't like his job are—he gets no paid vacation unless he threatens to quit, his job is dirty and hard, and he doesn't like the caliber of people he works with."[45]

The man himself expresses his frustration, not only by his determination to save his children from his fate, but also by his hopes and dreams of getting more enjoyable work. For example, Guest was informed by various automobile workers that: "When you get home from that place (Plant Y) you have no ambition. Unless it's a must and has to be done, you don't do anything. All I want is to get out of there."[46]

Walker was told by another assembly line worker: "When the plant was running only a few cars through an hour I used to install the whole front and back seat assemblies. But when the cars speeded up, I was put on the job of installing the rack that the front seat slides back and forth on and my job was broken up and simplified. I'd like to do a whole fender myself from raw material to the finished job. It would be more interesting."[47]

A common dream of escape is to have "a little business of my own" which Lipset and Bendix found to be the most commonly tried escape route, although the failure rate of these small businesses is extremely high. The automobile workers are no exception: "I'm going to go into my own business, I guess. If I get enough money salted away and times look good, I'll open up for myself. I think I can make out good that way. . . . You work just as hard, but it's for yourself." One remarked that he would like to have a little stationery store but, "it takes a lot of money to start, and I can't give up my seniority."[48]

In the automatic factory, a number of these complaints and sources of dissatisfaction have been removed. The plant is safer, more pleasant, and newer. The work is cleaner; in fact, a man may not need to get his hands dirty. Also, because of reintegration of work tasks, each worker has responsibility for a larger portion of the work and can understand how his part fits in with the whole production process. There is also some prestige attached to working in "the finest," "the most advanced," or the "most automatic" plant in the industry or in the area, which helps to restore the pride of even the lowest paid operator. Men in a recently automated plant of the Ford Company remarked about the new plant that it was "more interesting," "gives you more things to do," "you don't have to work so hard."[49]

A worker at a Burton factory commented: "The job is not nearly so monotonous. I like the changing around. You get a chance to run this machine and then you run that machine. They've made it a lot nicer for us than it used to be." Another worker responded: "I like to walk around and move around. That I can do on this job and I couldn't before. Just had to stand at one machine and do the same thing all day. You have to learn more machines, though, but that makes it interesting."[50] One of the employees stressed the aspect of salary. "Sure I like it better. It's a lot easier, I can tell you one thing—I'll last a lot longer on this job. I've worked 27 years for this company and I couldn't have held on to the old job much longer. It was too hard on me shoving those heavy blocks around. But this job's easy. I just watch these lights and push these buttons. Of course, I ought to have more money for this job."[51]

The reason this worker felt he should have more money for an easier job is that he believed he had more responsibility and he was aware of the increased productivity which automation makes possible. On both these counts, any worker is most likely to feel slightly disgruntled if he does not get higher pay. He likes the responsibility, on the whole, and he feels only that he is not given credit for exercising it or encouraged to take more. As one worker said: "I recognize that the company has to put out a lot of production to get back the money on their investment, but the general feeling among the men is that the company is getting a lot more out of increased production than the men are sharing."[52] Workers become aware that they are now being paid for "brain work" rather than physical work that can be measured in pounds, hours or pieces. "I get my best ideas about my job . . . when I'm in the can or at lunch, or on the way home. But under the incentive plan that isn't true work."[53] One worker emphasizes the increased responsibility. "On my old job . . . my muscles got tired. I went home and rested a little bit and my muscles were no longer tired. I also had nothing to worry about. On Number 4 [automated rolling mill] your muscles don't get tired, but you keep on thinking, even when you go home."[54]

A worker finds the greater frequency of shift work under automation disruptive to home life, which, as we have seen, is very much more important to him now than it was in the traditional, segregated family. He also objects to there being fewer rungs on the promotion ladder, even though this means that his superiors are fewer. He begins to realize that his wages are a result of the productivity of the system. He wants higher wages, but realizes he can do little as an individual to effect this, for "the system sets the pace for all" and he is integrated with a team. Correspondingly, he is less likely to believe that his union can deliver wage increases unless there is a corresponding increase in productivity. However, if he is safely in an automated plant, he has job security and usually higher wages than other workers, so he has little room for complaint on these grounds.

What the worker does want, however, is more recognition on the job. Some of these feelings are evident in complaints about the more impersonal and remote supervision usually associated with automation. "We were a lot closer to supervision when the mill started up. They wanted to help out. They asked questions and we made suggestions. X is one of the only ones who will talk about anything." "The higher-ups don't talk to us nearly as often as they used to. It's a funny thing, but they just don't seem to be the good fellows that we thought they were at first. They used to be really interested in the problems and come around and ask our advice. Now it is only when we have a breakdown that they come in and try to push us to get it fixed or give us dirty looks if they thought it was our fault. A lot of things that are wrong with that mill can be explained just by the attitude that is now built up beween the bosses and the men."[55]

When one man was asked what he would do if he were boss of the automated seamless pipe mill in which he worked, he replied: "I would go up to the man and say, 'This is *your* mill. I want you to feel that you're not in a prison, but you're in something that we are all in together and where we can all benefit. I want you to feel that you really want to work here—and I am willing to do anything I can to make you want to.' "[56]

The workers realize they are being asked to do brain work, that they have the capacity to do brain work, and they want the recognition and the status which they associate with such work. They feel that under the circumstances they have the right to be considered partners with management in the production process, and therefore should be consulted before, during, and after any change, as well as in day-to-day operations. It is interesting to observe that workers are in some ways beginning to function like management in relation to their jobs. The quotation above in which a worker said that he got his best ideas in the can or at lunch is highly reminiscent of the remark made by a member of top management in another survey. When asked how much leisure he had, he replied that it was hard to know since he was always thinking about the job. "I don't know whether I'm working or fishing."[57]

The lower echelons of white collar workers, often called "clerical workers" for statistical purposes, who once felt that their jobs offered flexibility, some control of their work, a good deal of intrinsic interest, and opportunities for promotion, are reacting to automation in the office in many of the same ways as men on a factory assembly line. These workers now have little control over work that has become monotonous. They are being subjected to time-and-motion studies, to shift work, and to sitting immobile at machines except during break periods—conditions with which the white collar worker never before had to contend. Such workers now complain of "being chained to the machine."[58]

An ex-clerical worker in a large public service organization in Montreal reports that the women who work there (mostly young girls) showed all the same symptoms of alienation and despair that we associate with the assembly line worker: arriving late, extending breaks and getting ready to quit early, and making such mistakes as putting paper clips in the machines in order to break the monotony and cause a little excitement. They never think of their work when away from it; instead, they dream of a better job, or of quitting to get more education. Some of them do leave to go back to school. Such typical remarks as, "Only fifteen minutes left. I hope I can survive" and "I hate this stupid building, this stupid desk and this stupid job" reveal the boredom and alienation felt by these girls. And the worker herself commented, "Several days before I quit, I had figured out how many seconds I had left to work. The brain work in many jobs has all but been eliminated. The girls find that their job is too close to a production line factory job. The work is too dull to be satisfying for them. They are all high school graduates and they find the work far below their capacity."[59]

Kassalow comments that, "Unlike the blue-collar worker, especially in industry, who has been 'living' with technological change most of his working life, the white-collar worker is unprepared for it, and its psychological impact upon him (or her) may be considerable."[60]

Of even greater importance, as demonstrated in the clerical worker's statement above, is the sense of deprivation relative to the aspirations and expectations encouraged by education and often developed by a middle-class background. As the proportion of clerical workers in the labour force grows, however, an increasing number of these workers will come from the working class, as a large majority always has. For them, "working conditions may not appear more onerous (or even as onerous) as those under which their blue-collar fathers and mothers worked—and continue to work. These are the comparisons that will probably be the most relevant to the new white-collar workers, and not the superior conditions that may have been enjoyed by other white-collar workers in the past."[61] To the extent that this is true, we may expect that the worker in the automated office will share the work attitudes and experiences of the worker in the automated factory.

The many influences we have discussed seem to be reducing hierarchical differences not only within the plant, but also in the society itself. The time-honoured cleavage between manual and nonmanual work, representing the class barrier between the working class and the middle class, is disappearing. Perhaps a new one will be constructed, say between upper and lower middle class, but at least the old wall is coming down.

7

Organizational Relationships

We can now consider the new worker in his relationships to the major institutions of which he is a part: his union, his industry, his community. Institutions are notoriously subject to cultural lag. What new problems does the emerging worker pose for these organizations, and what new solutions does he offer?

Union Problems: Factory Workers

There is evidence, some of which we have cited, to show that union power and prestige has been weakened, in the post–World War II period, and that until recently unions had ceased to grow and were even declining in membership. This was at least partly caused by the changing composition of the labour force which now includes more service, white collar, and professional workers than before; these groups are hard to organize, at least by traditional methods and appeals. In Britain, where white collar unions have grown almost as rapidly as unions in extractive industries have shrunk, union membership represents about 40 per cent of the nonagricultural work force and has fluctuated very little since

1948. In the United States, at least up to 1966, membership stood at 28 per cent, a fair drop from the high point of union organization in 1945 when 35.5 per cent of the American labour force (nonagricultural) were in unions.[1] In Canada, where the picture was comparable to that in the United States, there has been very recently an upswing, for reasons we will discuss later. However, white collar resistance to unionization, higher in the United States than in Canada, may be partly responsible for any decline in membership that occurred before or is now occurring in the two countries.

Another reason contributing to reduced membership is that, whereas workers once felt that their only hope of improving their wages and working conditions lay with a strong union, since the Second World War, management has tried, through enlightened personnel policies, to exceed unions in keeping workers content. Workers also are now better educated to understand the world they live in and the effect of increased productivity on wages. Furthermore, as we have seen, their awareness of working-class identity and that their interests and those of management are opposed is much diminished in the mass consumption, technologically advanced society.

Unions, being political organizations, have the problem of persuading the membership that the union is effective and useful. They must show, continually, such improvement in the lot of the workers that workers will continue to support and follow the union leaders. This problem has been made vastly more difficult by technological change. To keep pace with the rising expectations of wage earners and with the rising cost and standard of living, unions must press for higher wages. On the other hand, if they raise the cost of labour too much, industry has an incentive to introduce automation or other labour-saving machinery, thus threatening workers with loss of jobs, downgrading, early retirement, or at least loss of previous status and skills.[2] For this reason, and perhaps also because of the necessity to keep their incomes dependable in order to meet instalment payments, many workers seem more interested in job security than in wage increases, although this is not always the case.[3]

Raskin regards automation as the chief contributor to the weakening of the power of unions.

> The march of technology is like a pincer movement in its impact on unions. It eliminates large numbers of blue collar jobs in manufacturing and transportation, thus chipping away the bedrock of union enrollment. To the extent that new jobs are created, they involve hard-to-organize engineers, technicians, and white collar workers. That is one side of the nutcracker.

The other is the degree to which automation makes businesses invulnerable to strike harassment. When push buttons and electronic control devices regulate every operation from the receipt of raw materials to the loading of finished goods, a handful of non-union supervisors and clerks will be able to keep acres of machines producing in the face of a total walkout by unionized factory crews. . . . Even with existing production methods, our ability to make goods is so much greater than our ability to market them that most major industries can satisfy all the consumer demand of a prosperous year by operating their plants eight or nine months.[4]

An example of automation's effect on strikes occurred at the Clarkson plant of British American Oil in September, 1965. Six hours before the strike deadline, the staff and management took over the plant from workers in a show of force, proving that they could run at full production *without* workers.

Under these circumstances, of course, it becomes progressively difficult for unions to deliver impressive gains to their membership, and members become increasingly rebellious or indifferent. Automation also threatens the unions because industry-wide bargaining ordinarily does not take into account the difference in productivity between automated and non-automated plants. When there are different degrees of technology in an industry, workers in automated plants feel that they can gain more by bargaining at the plant level and tend to reject the industry-wide settlement, which may represent adequate wage compensation in less modern factories, but represents downgrading in more productive ones.

A further source of union weakness arises from changes in the union members themselves: the educated, younger workers are a new breed who hold self-conceptions, expectations, and attitudes that differ greatly from those of their leaders. Some may react to disappointment in their unions with alienation, others with rebellion. Seligman discusses the weakening of labour solidarity.

When automation comes, the consequences are such that dissension among unions is often the result. As jobs are abolished, occupations realigned, and tasks mechanized, a scramble ensues to see which union will exercise jurisdiction. . . . Mechanization and automation, however, have their most immediate effects on local plant problems, something that national bargaining can deal with but tangentially and ineffectively. The consequence is a dissatisfaction in the ranks that frequently leads to a rebellion against the international officers. Although Gleason may obtain a settlement he thinks is "the greatest in the history" of the I.L.A., the rank and file believe otherwise, and they strike all the ports along the Gulf and East Coast. Local union leaders decide to negotiate their own agreements in order to deal with local work conditions.[5]

In the United States in 1966, 11 per cent of the agreements reached between labour and management, *with the help of federal conciliators*, were rejected by the members—the highest percentage in history. Also, during the past two years, the presidents of four of the biggest unions, whose members make up one-eighth of the AFL-CIO, have been voted out of office. The struggle of Walter Reuther to save his leadership was another example of the growing discrepancies between union members and their leaders.[6]

The same patterns are seen in European countries. During 1968 and 1969, a series of work stoppages in France, Italy, Germany, and the United Kingdom described as "wildcat" strikes seemed to represent the same kind of rejection by the rank and file of agreements reached at an industry or employers' association level. As in North America, the demand is for more concern with factory-level problems and for more local autonomy in unions.

There can be no doubt that agreements which are reasonable on a nation-wide or even regional basis may not apply to a local situation. In Germany, Austria, and Italy, for example, there are often thirty to forty per cent wage differentials. Levinson analyzes these events.[7]

> It is normal that demands for greater voice, direct participation and decentralization of power, which is the basis of the "youth rebellion" today and which unions are demanding within industry, will occur within the trade union structure itself. . . . What began in the last few years as a seeming rank-and-file reaction against centralized authority of a traditional kind, has refined itself into an expanding, seemingly spontaneous and intuitive movement for greater self-determination and local authority to maximize local situations. Young workers in the most modern chemical process plants are not going to be satisfied with wages fixed in conformity with the productivity and earning of less modern establishments or in moribund industries. The task will be to secure a proper balance between social and local interests, which today is lacking.

1966 was a record year for industrial conflict in Canada; 1967 showed a slight improvement, but by 1968, relations had deteriorated to the 1966 level, involving over five million man-days lost. Most observers have made analyses of the situation which support our thesis of what can be expected of the young, educated worker, within the union and in the society. The *Monetary Times* speaks of labour as being in a "mood of unmatched militancy" and goes on to say:

The younger workers are those with more education, different values, no background of unemployment and with many alternate job opportunities. . . .

Surveys have shown that it is primarily the younger workers who are responsible for the new wave of militancy. They are, on the whole, more aggressive and readier to take strike action than older employees.[8]

In the same vein, Crispo and Arthurs, in a paper entitled, "Industrial Unrest in Canada: A Diagnosis of Recent Experience," prepared for the meetings of the Canadian Political Science Association and the Canadian Law Teachers Association in June 1967, made the point that: "To begin with, much of the unrest is characterized by militancy that is less the product of labour leadership than the spontaneous outbreak of rank and file restlessness."[9]

A good many of the ideas we have explored and attempted to find empirical evidence for are mentioned in this paper: educational differences between new and old workers, which mean that unions cannot count on automatic support from rank and file; mobility opportunities and affluence, which make workers less willing to accept compromise; and the weaker position that many unions find themselves in, partly because of these internal rifts. We would add to these analyses the findings on the effects on political attitudes caused by simply staying in school longer: the subjective sense of competence, the greater persistence in keeping informed on issues, and the increased egalitarianism. Affluence or rising income and occupational levels support the same attitudes. These attitudes are consistent, where dissatisfaction with work or rewards exist, with militancy. We would also like to add the importance of consumption norms in contributing to industrial unrest: this "desire for more," whether we like it or not, seems to be an important part of the structure of our economy. Unfortunately, we cannot have the advantages of this urge without its disadvantages.

These kinds of internal rifts are both a source of weakness for unions and the sign of a new militancy which may lead to increased labour strength. The same can also be said of union rivalry, such as that between the Confederation of National Trade Unions and the Canadian Labour Congress in Canada. It seems wasteful and destructive in a particular local situation, but has perhaps been responsible, at least partially, for rapid growth in union membership.

The 1965 gain of 9.3 per cent was the highest annual increase in union membership in Canada since 1952, when it jumped by 11.4 per cent. The total union membership at that time was 1,735,000, representing 24.5 per cent of the labour force. The *Financial Post* estimated that the gain was a result of the expansion of the labour force, near full employment, and vigorous organizational efforts, particularly on the part of automobile workers (the union with the greatest growth that year). Also, the CNTU competition with the CLC caused both to sharpen up organizational drives. Union membership did not change in 1966, but in 1967 was up 10.6 per cent over 1966, to a total of 1,921,000.[10]

In any case, there are signs now of a new upsurge in unionism and a new militancy, based, we expect, on quite a different philosophy than the traditional union organizer had in mind. The young, better-educated workers will not accept authority based on particularistic criteria, that is, a man's proven loyalty to the union, his early experience as a union fighter, and his emotional and ideological attachment to the past. These things are largely meaningless to young men who did not live through the organization struggles and the depression of the thirties.[11] On the contrary, through their longer experience in the school system, the young workers have had training in universalistic criteria. If we accept the findings of Inkeles's study of the modernization of man, we can assume that they believe in rationality, the overriding importance of technical competence, the rule of objective standards of performance, and the principle of distributive justice.[12] We would suppose that these criteria are being applied to union policy and structure by younger workers. If so, union practice must often be found wanting. We have already mentioned that old-timers in the unions feel themselves threatened also by the "experts" they have had to hire to deal with specialized areas. These highly educated specialists bring the same universalistic criteria to bear on union problems. It is no wonder that the old-timers feel beleaguered.

Union Problems: Office Workers

Sturmthal points out that, "With the possible exception of Japan, all industrial nations seem to share the American experience that white-collar workers are more difficult to organize into unions than blue-collar workers, and probably (although we made no special study of this) that women are less inclined to join unions than men."[13]

Given the rise in number of women employed and the increase in the proportion of white collar workers, the lack of participation must pose a serious problem for unions, for, as Sturmthal goes on to say: "The

danger confronting the movement [labour] is, of course, not its extinc-
tion, but rather the possibility that it may fail to grow with the growth
of the labor force. Most important, organized labor may be kept out of
the most dynamic sectors of the economy and thus lose some of its
vitality."[14]

However, this seven-nation study of white collar unionism shows that,
in spite of difficulties, organization of white collar workers is possible,
that it is being done, and that it is easiest in countries where blue collar
workers are already highly organized and the principle of unionism
generally accepted, such as in Sweden and Austria. Great Britain is somewhat behind these two, the United States lower still. In all countries
studied, public employees more readily join unions than workers in
private industry.

To speak of "white collar" as though it referred to a coherent group
sharing all-important characteristics, is largely a fallacy, of course. This
category includes professionals, top, middle, and lower managers, independent business men, technical and paraprofessional workers, secre-
taries and salespeople, file clerks and punch-card machine operators. As
we have said, only the lowest level of clerical worker in large organizations concerns us here and, according to Sturmthal's seven-nation study,
this is the group most susceptible to unionization. The reasons are fairly
clear: the effects of automation, such as job insecurity, impersonal,
monotonous work, and lack of opportunities for advancement incline
this group to collective action, since, unlike the higher level white collar
worker, they cannot see much chance of improving their lot individually.
In addition, the study suggests that "white collar groups whose status is
primarily based upon tradition and whose position in the plant (and
consequently in society) is declining are more susceptible to unionism
than groups whose status is confirmed or enhanced by the new technology
and labor market balance."[15] Finally, the study advances the possibility
that to the extent that these clerical workers come from blue collar
homes, they may have a "union attitude," which makes them easier to
organize, although this may not hold true for women.

We may assume, then, that union membership of the lower levels of
white collar workers will increase. What can we expect to result?

Not all white collar workers want the same things. Among professionals, for example, teachers, nurses, or engineers, one of the interests in
unionism (which is not very strong) is in maintaining professional
standards and the position of the profession vis-à-vis employers. This
interest is found in diminishing degrees all the way down the white collar
occupational hierarchy and differs from the way the semiskilled worker

feels about his work, although this concern is shared by skilled workers. Another characteristic of white collar workers, likely to affect unions and managers, is their expectation that work should offer both interest and challenge. When they join unions, then, these issues will be ones they expect the union to push. They also seem to be more concerned with vacations, sick leave, insurance, and stock-sharing programs than are blue collar workers. Beyond these issues, however, there is little difference between blue and white collar union demands.

But differences in attitude between blue and white collar workers are likely to cause trouble for unions. One is the greater reluctance of the white collar worker to strike, and the other is the effort to maintain traditional distinctions between themselves and blue collar workers. Most students confirm that white collar unions are loath to call strikes because their members have strong feelings against the use of the strike weapon and urge, instead, some kind of terminal arbitration machinery. Government workers, who are the easiest of all white collar groups to unionize, face, in some countries, legislation prohibiting strikes in the public service. This reluctance or inability to strike poses tactical problems for unions. As Guy Routh says of the British white collar unions: "The union leaders face a serious dilemma. They are generals of an army that shows up well on the parade ground but about whose willingness or ability to shoot there is much doubt. In his negotiations with the enemy, the general must rely on appeals to equity or bluff."[16]

On the other hand, the strike of New York City teachers in 1962 and 1963, the strikes of nurses and internes in Montreal in the last few years, and the U.S. postal strike of early 1970 suggest that this attitude previously shared by all levels of white collar workers may be changing.

The issue of maintaining traditional distinctions of pay and status in face of their functional meaninglessness is one which will eventually be decided on a rational basis, but meanwhile, it may cause considerable inter- or intraunion strife, depending on whether the white collar unions are organized in unions of their own or included in industry-wide unions. In either case, blue collar workers will fight the preservation of any special status for a group of workers whose work is so similar in skills and training to their own. Levinson reports that in Europe this problem is already being tackled by industry and unions.

Entire new categories and titles of skills are emerging which reflect the integrated manual and non-manual features of many new jobs. At Chemiker in Germany, Chemical Workers of ICI in the United Kingdom, Technicien in France, etc., controller, co-ordinator, maintenance worker are some of the new job headings being used which describe the post rather than the function or skill. Correspondingly, unions are demanding the integration of systems and levels of remuneration and conditions of work of manual and non-manual workers.[17]

Furthermore, white collar workers will exhibit the same kinds of attitudes which make the young, educated, and affluent factory worker cause difficulty for union leaders. They have not only the same education and comparable incomes, but also less working-class identification and more middle-class individualism. They are likely to be union supporters only so long as the union can deliver gains which they are not able to get for themselves. Unfortunately, whatever headaches white collar unionism may entail, the continued growth and viability of the union movement in all industrialized nations depends on the successful organization of these workers.

Industrial Problems

People become concerned about industrial relations, of course, when there is industrial conflict, and the general direction of effort is to promote agreement. It is our view, however, that strikes and other manifestations of labour-management disagreement are endemic to current assumptions about the roles and functions of labour and of management. There are two basic sources of conflict which are built into the system: the authority or control over work and the distribution of rewards. Since there is no rule of law which says exactly how these two things shall be divided between the contending parties and, since each group would, if it were possible, take all the control and all the rewards, conflict is inevitable in our system of industrial relations. Furthermore, we would argue that its expression is, under the circumstances, a sign of health, since only repression of the interests of one group or the other, or some rigid definition of the division of rewards and authority could eliminate conflict altogether. This argument does not imply that methods cannot be found to minimize the conflict or that there are not more constructive ways of expressing it. What we do want to emphasize is that it is not the conflict itself with which we should be concerned; it is what underlies it that is important. When there is evidence that work control and distribution of rewards are no longer realistic or just, and the conflict reaches such seriousness as to threaten the functioning of society itself, steps should be taken to treat the causes, not the effects.

Principal Issues in Industrial Conflict

From the point of view of this study, the two most important issues basic to industrial disputes in an age of automation and affluence are the conflict between management's right to organize work as quickly and efficiently as possible and the worker's right to control of his work; and the conflict between productivity and higher wages on the one hand and job security and unemployment on the other.

MANAGEMENT RIGHTS VERSUS WORKER RIGHTS

The struggle of the employer to determine the conditions under which he will pay for work and the struggle of the worker to determine the conditions under which he will sell his labour are as old as the first business transaction. Rapid technological change has simply made the conflict more acute and changed its formulation. And the nature of the new work environment, with its equalitarianism, its spread of responsibility on the one hand, and its basic insecurity due to continuous change on the other is leading to a new definition of the terms of trade.[18] Here we should emphasize that, although the modern worker is far more adaptable to technical change than is the traditional worker, such change represents a threat, insofar as a man may lose his job as a result of it.

A recent study by Wallen has defined succinctly this difference in the basic view of the work situation between labour and management.

> Business is often a conservative force on social questions. But when it comes to production, it is as radical as it can be. To the enterpriser feeling the sting of the competitive lash, there is no such thing as the status quo in technology or in the organization of production. He hunts feverishly for new materials, for new machines, for new ways of organizing work. When he finds them, he does not hesitate to uproot the established way of making or doing things in order to replace it with a better way.

> On the other hand, trade unionists and trade unions are often the pioneers, the radicals, in changing social institutions. But they tend to be the conservatives in their approach to changes in the methods of production. The status quo represents, they think, job security and certainty; change, presented in terms of the promise of a glowing

long-run future, is often accompanied by an uncomfortable, if not menacing tomorrow.[19]

The search for greater job security under conditions of continuous change has led, first, to an effort on the part of unions to establish the necessity for management to consult unions on work rules and imminent technical change. But even if the principle of consultation is accepted, it has the disadvantage of requiring continuous renegotiation. A second line of defense has been an effort to have the principle accepted that a man has a "right to his job," a property right in it, which may not be taken away from him or radically changed in nature without his consent.[20] This "professionalization" of labour deserves particular attention. Durand, in the OECD study of workers' attitudes to technical change, finds that trade unions in most Western countries are moving in this direction.

The effort to change a job into a career has become more realistic since automation, because the reintegration of work has made manual skills less important than theoretical understanding, which is applicable from one plant to another or one job to another. Another way in which jobs are becoming more like professions is that what a man sells is not so much his time (he may sit around in an automated factory doing very little except when something goes wrong or some decision has to be made) as his general knowledge, his capacity to understand a process, and his willingness to take responsibility. In his new feeling of equality, and in his search to improve his position and standard of living, what the worker wants is a career, which Foote defines as a "procession of statuses and functions which unfold in a more or less orderly though undetermined sequence in the pursuit of values which themselves emerge in the course of experience."[21] The issues of guaranteed annual wage (simply another word for salary), the right to a job, and the portable pensions may all be regarded as efforts to have the rights associated with a job become the property of the worker, so that he can take them with him wherever he goes.

An interesting new demand in this respect is the right to continuous training or "re-cycling." Claude Jodoin, in an article published in April, 1966, wrote that in an age of automation "training will become a factor in collective bargaining because it is so essential to the security of the worker."[22] Italian trade unions are demanding that there should be established, through multidimensional training, "an occupational qualification attaching to the person of the worker instead of to the job."[23]

To the extent that all these schemes make it more difficult to organize the work, managers may be expected to resist them as infringements of management rights. On the other hand, workers who are "professionals" might prove to be more responsible and easier to integrate into the work process.

RISE IN PRODUCTIVITY VERSUS JOB SECURITY

The second most important issue causing industrial dispute is the conflict between productivity and higher wages on one hand and job security and unemployment on the other. This conflict appears particularly acute in cases where technological changes, while increasing productivity per man-hour, lower total plant employment or make some skills obsolete.

It is unlikely that workers would be entirely happy about job security at the expense of a continued rise in productivity, and therefore, of wages.

Jamieson believes that rapid economic growth and expansion in Canada since World War II is responsible for more industrial conflict than any other factor. Rising prices and wage differentials between rapidly growing industries and slow growth industries, between high-wage and low-wage occupations in the same industry, between American and Canadian workers in the same union or industry have led to discontent often expressed in strikes. He notes that, "among the highly unionized industries in Canada strikes have been least prevalent in the one that has paid rates closest to those in the United States for several years, namely pulp and paper, and most prevalent in the one paying wages farthest below American standards, namely, coal mining."[24] Levinson also suggests that such differentials in Europe may have led to strikes by highly productive workers who are asked to accept wage agreements based on wage rates in less productive areas. Inequalities can lead to strikes by either low-paid or high-paid workers.

After all, the Canadian worker who reads American magazines and watches American TV and who works in Canadian subsidiaries of American companies and belongs to an international union with headquarters in the United States is subjected to continuous "demonstration effect"; that is, he compares himself and his standard of living, directly and realistically, with his American counterpart. Naturally, he wants the same things, since he participates, with only slight differences, in the general North American consumption pattern. The issue of wage parity with American workers in the same industry and in the same union has become a very difficult one, and it was necessary last year for the Federal Minister of Industry, C. M. Drury, to warn:

U.S. productivity is some 30 per cent above the level of Canadian productivity. This explains the fact that, on the average, U.S. wages are well above Canadian levels. . . . The sudden introduction of wage parity in a key industry, without being matched by comparable productivity growth for the economy as a whole, would tend to spread to other industries and to result in inflationary pressures, deterioration in the external trade balance, unemployment, then perhaps devaluation. . . .[25]

It would be very surprising indeed if Canadian workers were in the long run willing to accept less than parity with American workers. We can assume that the pressure for increased wages and for equalization of wages and benefits throughout Canada will continue. The work environment, the demonstration effect, the consumption norms, and the rising levels of education are all factors that influence Canadian workers to think in terms of parity with American workers. The same can be said of workers in Europe. The demonstration effect is now worldwide, through the mass media, as Kindleberger has pointed out. And since it is the United States that has the highest standard of living, it is with the American worker that parity is sought. Parity can only be achieved, however, if productivity steadily increases as a result of technological change. In that case, the worker will certainly attempt to protect his job through "professionalization" of work or some steps in that direction, which will involve a diminuation of management rights as now defined. It is unlikely that this struggle will be finished soon or that the contestants will be able to settle it among themselves.

CHALLENGES TO COLLECTIVE BARGAINING

The public in Canada and the United States has become increasingly concerned over the number and duration of strikes, particularly in public service industries, and a wage-price spiral in product industries. Although most contracts are quietly negotiated without public inconvenience, some of the most important issues, especially those associated with automation, seem beyond the reach of collective bargaining. J. T. Dunlop feels that the society has expected too much of collective bargaining and has burdened it with problems beyond the capacity of the participants to solve: for example, price stability, economic growth, full employment, and industrial peace.[26]

In spite of these difficulties, though, it seems likely that collective bargaining will continue to be an important tool for resolving the inevitable conflict of interests and the infinite details of industrial relations between workers and management. It may and ought to be improved, perhaps by becoming more centralized. Labour-management consultative committees may help to establish more rapport or to find solutions to problems before they have a chance to cause trouble. But the difficulty with all these solutions is that they assume that management and labour have private business of their own that does not concern the public and that, by leaving them to work out their problems alone, the interests of the rest of society will be served also. Only if they cannot settle their problems by themselves does the public (government) step in.

That this notion may be erroneous and unrealistic is demonstrated not only by the experience of many Canadians during the Seaway strike, the doctors' strike in Saskatchewan, or the Montreal Transportation Commission strike in Montreal, but also by a study of the steel strike in the United States which lasted from July 15 to November 7, 1959. R. L. Raimon found that in this case there were certain new conditions based on high productivity and affluence which challenge previous assumptions about industrial conflict.

> We have in the past assumed that (1) both labour and management have more to lose than to gain from interruptions to production. (2) When strikes or lockouts do take place, the hardships they themselves entail will be the chief instrument making for prompt settlement. Promptness is measured by the notion that the staying power of the parties will be less than the staying power of the public. These ideas are challenged by the following new conditions in the more affluent industries:
>
> (1) Technically advanced industries have an over-capacity to meet demand and operate most profitably at high or near-capacity production levels. Therefore, a company will show a greater profit if it works at near-capacity during half a year and shuts down the other half than if it must work at low levels all year round. A long strike may be a good thing for the company, especially if
>
> (2) Stockpiling is feasible. With the amount of warning usually necessary to the calling of a strike, buyers can buy all they need for a very long period.
>
> (3) Industry-wide bargaining makes it impossible for individual firms to resume operations and capture their rivals' customers during a strike.
>
> (4) Workers' incomes are high enough so that their staying power is as great as the public's. In 1958, despite the recession and the consequent infrequency of overtime earnings, the median earning of *wage employees* in steel exceeded the median income of American *families* in that year.[27]

Under these conditions, it is clearly possible that either party to a dispute may welcome, or at least passively accept, a strike and that both can outlast the public in withstanding the inconvenience. We must agree with Cardin that, "it is today a paradox that a system of industrial relations should be, for all practical purposes, based on the absolute liberty of the parties to the negotiation, and on bargaining within a perspective of private law in which only the interests of the opposing groups count."[28]

Community Problems

We have at various stages of this study referred to the new worker's probable relation to his political and social community. We have shown that he is likely to be more middle class in his life style and to be more conservative in political attitudes than the traditional worker. These trends will be reinforced by the influence of the white collar workers, who at the lower levels of skill and income, have always shared the life style and social attitudes of the middle class and who are now joining unions as their work experiences approximate those of semiskilled factory workers. In the circumstances, we would expect that workers, particularly in Canada and the United States, will tend to vote more conservatively and to resist efforts of their unions to affiliate with political parties or movements with a strong working-class bias.

Along with this conservatism goes a middle-class individualism, a strong sense of one's rights, an unwillingness to "be pushed around," an insistence on control of one's affairs which may cause trouble for governments and communities that have been accustomed to acquiescence or indifference on the part of workers. We think that the consequences of this relatively new attitude may be longer in coming because the worker feels less involvement in his social and political environment than in his economic one. On the other hand, the mobility of the modern worker and his separation from the support of the extended family will, eventually, make him dependent on such community services as nursery schools, medical clinics, and social clubs, and we should then see more workers and their families involved in the use of and support of these services. In addition, wars, racial conflict, or unemployment create a sense of urgency and community involvement as is shown in "block" organizations in American cities, in which citizens of the block organize for mutual aid and protection.

Problems of Integration

A central problem in an age of rapid technological change, of affluence, and of rising levels of education is integration: integration, as Drucker has said, of professional managers and professional specialists and, as Durand foresees it, of professional workers into the production process, and integration of all these with the general society.

Under mass production conditions, workers had their own working-class values in a working-class subculture; unions were a political expression of working-class values and needs. But now the working man in North America and elsewhere is less and less conscious of his affiliation with a working class. He is confident that the future looks reasonably bright for himself (barring world wars and depressions), and even more so for his children. His style of life and his work experience confirm a growing equalitarianism, in spite of certain obstacles erected by national societies. The attitudes of workers are undergoing change, but so far they have failed to find integrative roles for themselves in our vast middle class. And the apathy or rebellion in union ranks suggests that unions have failed to keep up with this change.

Specialization has been for some time characteristic of all parts of society. However, the nature of modern technology now requires that these specialists be reintegrated and organized into a smoothly functioning work force of independently responsible individuals. This development is taking place not only in automated factories, but in the professions as well. For example, the increasing demand for medical services which at first required the separation of the doctor's skills into many separate functions, divided among as many practitioners (the anesthetist, the radiologist, the lab technician, the physiotherapist, the psychologist, the surgeon), now requires the reintegration of all these specialists into hospital teams. Through organization, various combinations of these specialists must now act together to perform the functions once performed by the individual doctor. But their integrated activities make possible an efficiency, a level of proficiency, and a durability that the family doctor working alone could not provide. Most important, each member of such a team feels he makes a contribution and has a responsibility, and he recognizes that this is true of all other members too. This kind of integration of the worker is lacking in industrial relations at the present, but is what must come.

We believe that industrial plants must increasingly reflect on a social and psychological level what is happening on a functional level. If the mistake of a machine operator is as costly as that of a supervisor, then the operator's importance should be recognized, not only through wages, but also through increased responsibility for decisions and planning. Such integration, we believe, would go far to restore workers' interest in their job and to ease a source of strain in industrial relations that is likely to increase in the future.

Integration in our social environment as well is important if we are to avoid stress and conflict. Saul Alinsky's "Back of the Yards" movement and other efforts of disadvantaged groups to organize to rectify their wrongs and overcome their problems through their own efforts begin in groups where economic, social, and political problems are most severe. But the idea is widely accepted and available for any group which feels itself badly used by the society. If the poorest, most disadvantaged people of our North American society are now able and willing to organize to improve local conditions, our political and social institutions, as well as our economic ones, had better make some new assumptions. We should assume that the new worker will want to be involved in the planning and operation of his own community. Local school boards, city councils, and community welfare programs must cease to represent largely the middle class and must seek and provide for active participation of a much wider spectrum of social groups.

8

Structural Strains
and Dislocations

In this chapter, we turn from the description and analysis of changing environmental experiences and attitudes of the emerging worker to a consideration of what these changes mean when we look at society in more abstract and theoretical terms.

The Trend of Modernization

We have described the ways in which the younger, affluent, and educated worker differs from the traditional worker. While both live up to the "standard package" of home ownership, of having televisions, automobiles, vacations, and hobbies, they differ in their approach to dealing with their environment. The modern worker has, because of education, ways of dealing with reality which Inkeles refers to as "modernization"; a capacity for universalism (holding impersonal and objective standards), specificity (dealing only with those aspects of the situation and arguments logically relevant to it), independence (working alone without direct supervision), and achievement. Robert Dreeban maintains that these are a product of long immersion in modern educational organizations, that they are learned inadvertantly from such immersion, and that they may be more important to survival in the modern world than academic knowledge.[1]

These modernizing orientations are in turn reinforced by working in highly technical industries which themselves "teach" the workers how to use them. They are, of course, the orientations of bureaucracy and include a high degree of rationality, and they are necessary to functioning in and understanding a highly bureaucratized and rationalized society. We repeat, they are the product of education and of experience in such a society. They distinguish the modern worker from the traditional worker. They have many implications for the role of the modern worker in unions, in industry, and in the community, which we will deal with shortly. However, before doing so, we should describe the frames of reference and the social order which develop around the traditional worker and why they constrain and frustrate the modern worker.

The mark of the older working-class culture noted in many studies is that the orientations of its members were not universalistic and specific. Instead, they reacted to others in terms of their personal qualities and made allowances for their characteristics. They relied on family and friends for support and security and stressed sharing and loyalty to the group instead of competition. They had low aspirations. When these were coupled with such low levels of education that a great many workers were, in fact, functional illiterates, one can understand their total incapacity to deal with modern technological developments. Their attitudes, in fact, encouraged paternalism. Indeed, whether it was true paternalism, in the personalistic sense of that term, or the kind of corporate paternalism now a constituent part of Bulwarism, the worker was treated as though he were a child. In fact, we would go even further and note that, even within the structure of the unions with their highly oligarchical tendencies, the worker tended to be treated in the same way. To some extent, this attitude was appropriate, for such workers were not equipped either to understand or to function efficiently in modern industry. Authority was left to management and to union leadership.

The social structure which developed around such workers had to be one in which they were closely supervised, and given very little responsibility. This need for supervision, in turn, set up a complex hierarchy which inadvertently provided ways in which those workers with talent or education could work their way up. Their leaving the working group, however, left the rest of the work force rather uniformly helpless and nonresponsible.

Certain categories of workers should be exempted from these generalizations, particularly the skilled workers and craftsmen. They have almost always been better educated than other workers and more independent and affluent. Furthermore, one should understand that, even for the rest of the work force, our remarks are not intended to be a description of these workers, but to depict a tendency within them as a body, or among a sufficient number of them, to necessitate the kind of social organization which we have described.

With the increased technological complexity of modern industry, this traditional work force was left further and further behind. The gap between what they knew and what was required for managerial decisions widened even further and, with the widening, upward mobility became increasingly difficult. In addition, more and more members of management held college degrees.

Naturally, with this level of a work force, management felt that it had to make all decisions. True, this idea was also linked to management's possession of power and its ownership of the means of production, but it was also supported by the nature of the work force. Regardless of its etiology, it is clear that management did come to believe that it had the *right* to make all the decisions about production, sales, remuneration, and even workers' rights. The "residual rights" theory, still current and supported by much legal precedent, is based on the assumption that management has all original rights, with the exception of those specifically given away in collective agreements.

One can find a similar set of conditions in both the unions and the community. Unions, except for some, such as the printers' union, have been notoriously undemocratic, being ruled by extremely durable oligarchies of traditionalists. In the community, the traditional, blue collar worker is noted for his low level of participation in almost all activities. He belongs to almost no clubs or associations, he tends to be politically inactive, and he has certainly never been asked to appear on the boards of community institutions like hospitals.

This, then, is the picture of the institutional frames within which the modern, blue collar worker now finds himself. But times have changed. Many workers are now affluent, and an increasing proportion of the younger workers are well educated. The new worker brings to these older organizations new skills and new standards of competence. He has a highly modern orientation, a different sense of self, and a much more equalitarian and liberal attitude toward his relationships and responsibilities to others. He does not accept the factory system devised for the traditional worker. He finds the fragmentation and routinization of tasks devised by men like Taylor to make him efficient, repulsive and demeaning. He is dissatisfied with his work, and increasingly challenges the competence of foremen and the rights of managers.

As we have indicated elsewhere, surveys have shown that the more educated the blue collar worker, the more likely he is to be dissatisfied with his work, and the more he will want to make some of the decisions connected with his job. If he works in an automated or semiautomated plant, he will reject the obsolete competence of the older workers and foremen, feeling that his part of the job is as important as anyone else's. He turns away from work as a source of satisfaction and expects his home, his family, and his leisure to meet his needs for recognition, status, and creative outlets. Whatever the meaning of work to the traditional worker, it is clear that to the modern worker it is merely the means to a high standard of living. This worker has then become, or is becoming, alienated from society by the major way in which he is made part of it. When these workers do have the chance to participate in decision-making, as they do in some continuous process industries, they express satisfaction with and involvement in their work.

The experience of the modern worker in the union has also been stressful. Evidently, he has little respect for the oldtime union leaders; he has not experienced the early battles fought by the unions and which made their reputations, nor does he respect very much the values so important to them, such as loyalty and hard work. Instead, he is likely to apply the bureaucratic standards he has internalized with his longer schooling, valuing the rationally competent and technologically knowledgeable man. He, himself, probably has these skills and feels himself more competent than his union leader. Furthermore, he is not satisfied with the goals which the older leader brings to collective bargaining. In short, he rejects the leader and his policies, and there is some evidence that this dissatisfaction provokes the modern worker to lead wildcat strikes; or he may favour a different kind of participation in the union, replacing loyalty to the union and regular attendance at meetings with competence in committees. Whereas the older leader was a mass politician, using and abusing the mass meeting to achieve his ends, the modern worker will prefer bureaucratic politics, the meetings of experts, and the effective committee.

Finally, the modern worker *may* become disenchanted with the community in which he lives, for he certainly is not respected by the community institutions which he uses. Neither hospital nor school boards, social agencies, nor recreation commissions have many representatives from among the workers. Though the workers are probably the principal users of these institutions, they have almost nothing to say about how they are run. These institutions were also developed to serve the traditional worker who was thought to be, and probably felt, incompetent to direct them. Of course, the result is that most of these institutions are run according to the interests of the middle class who dominate them, or at least according to what the middle class considers good for the workers. That this can be both fallacious and unjust has been shown in a number of instances. Public hospitals, whose primary clientele are workers, are built in areas of the city relatively inaccessible to them. If the workers *had* been members of these boards, such locations would not have been chosen.

Our point, then, is that the modern, blue collar worker, in spite of his competence, his high aspirations and expectations, is unable to find a place in his society and feels alienated from his work and from his union. This frustration can only produce dissatisfaction and restlessness.

The Status System

In 1953, Peter Drucker wrote an article called "The Employee Society" in which he described modern industrial enterprises as status systems.[2] He was referring to the fact that rewards (pay) are allocated, not in terms of the contribution of the worker, but in terms of his relative status in the system. He argued that management had the power of deciding how the profits of the enterprise would be redistributed; that is, how much would go to each status position. Pursuant to this, he maintained that it is the function of labour to challenge management in this right of redistribution. What is particularly valuable for us is his conceptualization of the work world as a status system. It focuses attention on the mechanism and criteria for allocating people to statuses, as well as the ways of granting prestige. Status distinctions, like those between blue collar workers, white collar workers, and management, have in the past represented prestige levels within industry paralleled by differences in pay and usually life styles, education, skills, sex, age, and ethnicity— differences which functioned to legitimate the status system and consequently the distribution of power and the redistribution of profits.

That these differences affect status is made strikingly clear by the findings of sociologists that management and labour are differentiated in terms of class and ethnicity, so that in North America one often finds that management is primarily in the hands of white Anglo-Saxon Protestants, while labour, particularly unskilled and semiskilled labour, is largely composed of other ethnic groups. This is the grounds for the complaint of the French Canadians that industry in Quebec is dominated by the English. This same differentiation seems to be true wherever industry is introduced from the outside and even, to some extent, where the industry is developed, owned, and operated by members of the native population.

Similar differences exist in the different levels of labour, although these are usually not based on class, but rather on ethnicity, sex, age, or personal relationship. Though these differences were clearly the result of ethnic and class nepotism and inimical to a democratic ideology, they had the important *latent* function of legitimating the power and advantages of management by *implying* that this was part of the natural order.

The question is, why do the participants accept these differences? Partially, it is because they feel that the people occuping distinctive statuses *are* in some way fundamentally different. In societies like India, caste differences are considered to be part of the divine and natural order. In the West, these differences are justified by the principle that property confers power and privilege; that is, owners of an enterprise have the right to say whom they will hire, for what job, and under what circumstances. Although the logic of this has become rather tenuous in a society where managers are for the most part employees, not owners, the argument is still used. However, except for those in the upper echelons, it is probably not really accepted.

Today, education is probably the most important legitimation for these status differences. The distinctions between white collar worker, blue collar worker, and management have for a long time been supported by major differences in their levels of education. Therein men could find the reason for the superiority of others. This is why education has become, in the minds of North Americans, the most important avenue to success. Men "understand" why others get ahead in terms of their superior education and, if they have hopes for their children, they are adamant about giving them a "good" education. In fact, education has become so closely associated with status that people expect an increase in education to result in a better job, and that more respect and deference will be given them.

Life style provides somewhat the same justification, though its influence is more subtle and indirect. It has the double function of legitimating and symbolizing status. When men live differently they are thought to be different, so that a man with a bigger income and a much more luxurious style of life is somehow thought to be a better man. Thus, as long as the manager had a dramatically different life style from that of the worker, far from causing dissatisfaction, it probably helped convince the worker that there was a real difference between them and that the manager was a better man. When this is no longer true, the status difference, which was supported and articulated by differences in life style, is no longer valid.

But now, with rising levels of education and affluence, both these differences are disappearing and with them the legitimation for the differences in power and privilege.

Among younger workers, there is certainly a very small educational gap between the blue collar and the white collar worker, and a great reduction in that between the blue collar worker and the manager. The distance between a grade school education and a college education is, psychologically and cognitively, far greater than that between a high school and a college graduate. Often the man with the grade school education is actually a functional illiterate, not accustomed to thinking in abstractions nor to using printed matter. He is thus clearly distinct from the manager with college and even high school education. This was the condition of what we have called the "traditional" blue collar worker, a condition suitable for the status system we find in industry.

Now, increasingly, workers have a high school education. Such workers are not likely to see much difference between themselves and the white collar workers (except that the latter may not be as well paid), and they feel able to speak to the managers. They will, in other words, be far less willing to concede that the status differences are justified. Furthermore, they will expect that their greater abilities, arising from their greater education, will be recognized. In a multitude of ways (like the criteria of competence he uses, his appreciation of the world, and his cognitive and social skills), today's younger worker is a different man. Being different, he will need new modes of participation and new sources of satisfaction. There is no indication that a system grounded on the traditional worker provides such outlets or satisfactions.

With these two effects in mind, we can say that, in the most affluent and highly educated sectors of the economy, workers (and, to some extent, managers) will tend to reject the status system and be restive in its confines.

If we accept Peter Drucker's thesis that modern industry is a redistributive system geared to social status, with the power of redistribution in the hands of management, then the erosion of the legitimacy of this system will have serious effects. The disappearance of differences in education and life styles which legitimated the status system means that, unless we are prepared for continued, serious, structural strains, that system too must change.

We would also note that the privilege of power is linked to these status differences and that accordingly the exercise of power is legitimated in terms of its acceptance. To the extent that this status system disappears, management, which up to now has been seen as the only group with the right to redistribute profits and to exercise control over the work, will be increasingly challenged by the unions or the workers themselves. Whether the challenge comes from the unions will depend on whether it is traditional members or modern workers who achieve dominance. Where the former is the case, we may expect wildcat strikes and local rejections of the settlement brought back by their leaders, for the modern worker will not be satisfied with the control over redistribution achieved by the traditionalist leaders and, probably, not even with the share of the profits they bring back.

To sum up, we have suggested that the effect of affluence and increased education on the status system of modern industry is to erode the legitimacy of this system. This, in turn, means that the involvement of the modern, affluent, highly educated worker is weakened and is unsatisfactory to him.

We predict that this dissatisfaction will be expressed in a claim for increased control over the redistribution of profits and over the production process itself. Unions which contain both traditional and modern workers will experience intense internal struggles for power. Where the traditional group is in power in the union, the other group will lead wildcat strikes and rejections of settlements.

The Advantaged and Disadvantaged Groups

Studies of slums, of schools, of colleges, and of prisons point to another type of strain in modern society that has been created by technological-economic-educational change. This strain arises out of two interconnected and simultaneous developments: the increasingly high standard of life, education, and performance and the resulting widening gulf between the advantaged and disadvantaged. The high standard has become the unit by which every man measures himself and, against this standard, the disadvantaged see themselves as failures. This finds its starkest consequence in the hard-core unemployed who constitute a serious social problem for the nation. There is, however, an even more pernicious result: the loss of hope for the young and their alienation from the social system in which they are involved.

The classic explanation of this structural dislocation is offered by the sociologist Robert K. Merton who points out that increasingly, in modern mass society, people are being presented with goals, but denied access to the means for achieving them.[3] He specifically refers to the income and life-style goals presented in the mass media, and to the fact that disadvantaged groups, such as unskilled workers and ethnic and racial minorities, simply could not get the education and/or connections necessary to reach these goals. Merton suggests that the person who faces this problem could deal with it in a number of ways; for example, he could deny the goals (become a hippie), reject the means (become a criminal), or reject both the goals and the means (become a revolutionary). Whatever the choice, he proposes that such a frustrating situation would lead to a loss of faith in the validity of the social norms and that anomie or moral lawlessness would ensue.

The applicability of this theory to juvenile delinquency is obvious. The slum boy who is taught to want what everyone else wants (the effect of ideological equalitarianism and a mass media society), but finds himself a failure at school and unable to get a good job, bands together with others of kindred fate to form the juvenile gang. Such gangs are noted for their rejection of social values by engaging in both destructive and hedonistic activity. By these actions, the delinquent is saying that he knows that he will not be rewarded for participation in the society. He has become alienated.

Merton's theory may also apply to a range of other phenomena such as high school and college rebellions, convict apathy, and perhaps even rebellion in and alienation from the union. In these cases, people often feel that there is little or no relationship between their present activities and their future prospects. Arthur Stinchcombe comments in his *Rebellion in the High School* that those high school students who rejected their role as students and insisted on adult privileges were those who felt that what they were learning and doing in school would do nothing to help them in later life. These students, who were mostly lower-class boys and middle-class boys who were failing, did not feel that participation in the school life offered any advantage; they rejected their role of adolescents and students, and demanded that they be treated as adults.

A similar interpretation could account for college rebellions, except that here the rebellious students are of the middle class. (The lower-class students feel that they have already accomplished a goal and are quite satisfied.) The middle-class students tend to reject the competitive system since they feel that, even though they struggle, they will not be able to improve their positions; the system condemns them to holding the same status their fathers hold. Finding no advantage in continued competition, they, too, reject the system and the role the system assigns to them. They demand adult status, which often means a demand for participation in the government of the university.

Something of the same process is at work when the young business school graduate or engineer feels disgruntled because he is not given enough recognition and responsibility right away.

Our interpretations of college rebellions and the difficulties of junior executives may be tenuous. They are presented simply to illustrate the ways in which rebellions can be generated. The explanation of slum delinquents and high school rebels has, however, been firmly established. In each instance, the boy does not believe that his participation will result in the kind of life style which the system promises or which he has come to believe he should have. His attitude is, of course, a product of his experience and of the standards of society; and it will be determined by conditions in that society, as well as the height of the standard applied.

Paralleling this development is another, arising out of the increasingly technological nature of work. Jobs are clearly becoming more complex and require more training. Computer programming is a case in point— a poor job of programming is absolutely useless. The growing gap between unskilled and skilled work makes it increasingly difficult for the novice to learn on the job. Unlike the boy on the farm who can copy his father, albeit poorly, and still know that he is useful, the son of a computer programmer, since he lacks the necessary training, simply cannot do what his father does, and therefore feels useless.

This development makes most entry jobs increasingly unpromising. They are not ways of learning the business. They tend to be dead end. To accept them is either an admission of failure or, since these jobs are increasingly occupied by married women returning to the labour market, they may be regarded by boys as jobs for females only. As a consequence, working-class boys in school find it more and more difficult to see a meaningful relationship between what they are studying and what they will be doing on the first job. A Canadian study of a high school indicated that many working-class boys definitely felt this way.[4] Middle-class children do not feel quite so alienated because they see high school as the preparation for college where they *will* learn the skills of modern work. Yet they, too, share and clearly resent the feeling of being useless and being unable to participate seriously in their society. They, too, have tendencies to reject the system and the role it assigns to them and demand adult status.

With this perspective in mind, we would argue that the increased levels of affluence and education have raised the standard by which a man measures himself; at the same time, these increased levels are established by the new workers themselves. For example, a study of English workers showed that the educational requirements of a job were those of its last occupant, and that other things being equal, the man with the highest education tended to get the job. The higher the standard, the more the uneducated man will be at a disadvantage, and the greater the chance that he will anticipate failure.

Rising standards of living and education tend to be accompanied by rising levels of expected competence or performance. Spread by mass media and human dreams, these standards are accepted by more and more men. They become shared by the schools, they creep into job qualifications and the thinking of personnel men, and then become part of the picture of the successful or adequate man projected in stories, television, and movies.

Under these conditions, disadvantaged groups will tend to reject schooling, noting its lack of relevance for the entry jobs they will take. They develop what Paul Goodman has called "reactive stupidity" (an emotional incapacity to learn and express their feelings) and, in Arthur Stinchcombe's terms, show "expressive alienation," rejecting their role as students and insisting on adult activities like sex, driving cars, smoking, and drinking. This is, of course, the springboard for entry into the corps of the underemployed or the hard-core unemployed. Being ill-educated, they cannot compete for good jobs and are not adaptable enough to avoid obsolescence.

Conclusions

We have, then, three broad developments arising out of changes in education and affluence which result in structural strains and/or dislocations within our society. First, the working man becomes transformed by increased affluence and education in such a way that he can and wants to play a new role in his work place, his union, and his society. However, since these institutions are geared to the relative incompetence of traditional workers, there is no way in which the modern worker can play a new role. Even in automated plants, this problem is not solved because, although the worker feels he has more responsibility and is expected to think, he does not feel that he obtains the recognition and status he deserves. He is, therefore, frustrated and dissatisfied, rebellious when he can be, often alienated when he cannot. This is probably one of the underlying reasons for recent labour unrest and militancy.

The strains arising out of the worker's being a new man in an old society are amplified by the gradual deterioration of parts of that society. The status distinctions based on education and life style (which were the basis for the rights of management and the difference in power and pay between management and the workers) are disappearing. Therefore, in the eyes of the worker, these managerial rights and the manager's much greater power and pay are no longer justified. The worker thus demands more control over his own work, pay more equal to the manager's, and he challenges management's rights to decide these things unilaterally.

Finally, the new worker sets a new and higher standard for work and living. These higher standards are more difficult for disadvantaged groups to reach, with the result that more of them fail and many of their children reject even the effort to achieve them. Thus, while the modern worker becomes alienated through the frustration of his needs and the meaninglessness of work, the traditional worker becomes alienated by the seeming impossibility of success. He then becomes dislocated from the structure of his society to become part of the underemployed or hard-core unemployed.

Elsewhere, we have pointed out that some environmental influences, such as affluence, mass consumption norms, mobility, and an instrumental view of work tend to ease some of these strains, particularly for the modern worker. In this chapter, we have deliberately emphasized the potential sources of conflict and difficulty, particularly for industrial relations, because it is to these areas that public policy should address itself.

9

Solutions

We have been concerned throughout with the importance and the necessity in an affluent, technologically advanced society of the adoption of mass consumption norms by all members of the society. Ambition, the desire to reach a higher and higher standard of living and to achieve a life style worthy of respect—these motives, far from being reprehensible, are essential. They, plus the conditions that exist under automation, hold out the possibility of freeing man from his ancient servitude to debilitating physical labour and to degrading social classification.

At the same time, we must recognize that the affluent mass consumption society contains a number of anomalies and contradictions, as Galbraith has pointed out. For instance, we have not maintained the social balance (a kind of technological ecology) with the result that our economic investment in private goods, like automobiles and television sets, exceeds our public capacity to deal with their social consequences. This is a serious problem, but we will not linger on it, since Galbraith has dealt with it in considerable detail. Instead, we would draw attention to a more subtle, but more far-reaching and potentially explosive contradiction in our affluent society.

An Outdated Philosophy

The development of our socioeconomic system was strongly influenced by the problem of scarcity. This provided the basic "interest" which explained why men acted as they did and made their behaviour predictable. It gave moral justification to conflict of interest and institutionalized the competitive or adversarial system as the best way of allocating men and resources. We have extended this competitive ideology into law, into labour relations, into the market place, and indeed, into love, and have consistently assumed that the best man would win and that the desire to win would make the world go round. Veblen's "conspicuous consumption," motivated by competitive accumulation of goods, fits this view also. The competitive system seems an ideal one for a developing industrial society, since it justified inequality, developed entrepreneurs, and legitimated work and saving. It was, in other words, functional to the problems of that kind of a society. It makes almost no sense in a postindustrial, affluent society.

When men grow up in a society where they have almost everything they need and want, where possessions and their acquisition can no longer justify one's existence, where poverty is clearly senseless, the acquisitive, competitive urge atrophies. Simply expressed, a sated man is not motivated by hunger, and in an affluent society, an institutional system based on scarcity is an absurdity.

Thus, while more consumption seems essential to the mass production necessary to a high standard of living, it seems to contain the seeds of its own destruction. Hopefully, once we have learned how to be affluent, we can continue to produce without the spur of scarcity. Even so, we will still need new values, motivations, and sources of involvement and satisfaction.

We can see the beginning of a reaction to the competitive system among certain groups of middle-class college students. They reject both the standards of competition and consumption, claiming that they are not interested in the promotion ladders or in high income. Many of the most talented try living in communes and turn down good jobs in the industrial world. At the moment, however, deep forms of alienation seem limited to the middle-class young. The affluent, educated worker does not reject this socioeconomic system. He wants to share in it and to win recognition and control. The affluent society has given him some freedom.

Freedom and Responsibility

But freedom for what? Leisure pursuits and avocational creativity have sufficed as reasons for the existence of aristocracies in the past, but such groups, if they were not to be corrupted, had always a sense of involvement and responsibility to the community of which they were a part. If we are about to witness an aristocracy of the common man, how can he achieve this same sense of involvement and responsibility?

The simple and infantile desire for more and more is clearly present in most people, but it is not all that is there. A man cannot be satisfied simply to consume endlessly; to get and not to give. His sense of worth and dignity requires that he give something in the bargain. Work, when it was the measure of a man, could be also a gift of himself, the most important thing he could offer. Therefore, in the industrial bargain, a man's labour was regarded, and not only by Marxists, as contributing real value, if not the true value of products. But as machines take over more functions, as the meaning of work changes to an instrumental one, what can a worker contribute which will maintain his self-respect, his sense of belonging to and contributing something of real value to the work environment and to the society?

Bright and Walker, in seperate studies, found that workers appreciate the added sense of responsibility over a greater span of the operation that occurs with automation. And both found the common complaint that, although the workers had ideas for improving the productivity of their machines, they were rarely asked for advice. Many observers of adolescent unrest believe that the young person's sense of being without function or value in the larger society is partly to blame for his alienation and rebellion against its values. An example from industry of these untapped resources is the case of eight girls employed in the paint room of a toy factory who were allowed, after many complaints, to arrange the work flow in what they thought would be the most efficient way. Within three weeks, these girls had increased their productivity from 30 to 50 per cent above the level expected by production engineers when they themselves had planned the work flow. Instead of the work moving at a constant pace all day as the engineers planned, the girls simply devised a varied pace which prevented their becoming either bored or tired.[1]

The argument is often raised that workers do not really want more responsibility. Although this may be true in individual cases, statistically it is not, a fact demonstrated by two surveys made by the Survey Research Center—one of 580 office workers, the other of 5,700 production workers in heavy industry.[2] The results for office workers were:

Employees making no decisions who would *not* like to make any	11 per cent
Employees making some decisions who would *not* like to make more	13 per cent
Employees making no decisions who would like to make some	30 per cent
Employees making some decisions who would like to make more	46 per cent

This shows that 41 per cent of the workers feel that they make no decisions, although 76 per cent would like to make some or more.

The majority of the factory workers (68 per cent) felt that they had little or nothing to say about how their jobs should be carried out, but 65 per cent of them were convinced that the work would be more efficiently done if the men had more chance to make suggestions about such things as design, setups, and the layout of the work. When asked why the men did not make more suggestions, the following responses were given:

Men do not get credit for suggestions	50 per cent
Top management will not use suggestions men make	28 per cent
Foremen will not use suggestions men make	23 per cent
Other men do not think a man should make suggestions	11 per cent
Men do not know where to make suggestions	10 per cent
Men do not know what suggestions to make	7 per cent

The important statistic to note here is the tiny proportion who believe they or their fellows have nothing to contribute and the large proportion who feel frustrated in their desire to take some responsibility for their work.

It seems obvious that we now have workers whose increasing general education equips them to handle the kind of abstract problems represented by automatic factories. They can, therefore, *think* and will be expecting to use this capacity. Furthermore, from the point of view of productivity and the full development of human resources, means must be found to utilize the capacities of workers for involvement and responsibility in the productive task. As we observed at the end of chapter 7, the social organization of industrial plants ought to reflect the changes in their technical organization, that is, the spreading of responsibility and a flattening of hierarchies. Including workers in the work-planning process is a realistic recognition of their responsibility in technologically advanced plants, and it also may help to make work meaningful and to ease frustrations which will otherwise undoubtedly lead to individual grievances and industrial disputes.

As we saw in the last chapter, the status system has been legitimated heretofore by the common assumption that class or social differences represent basic differences—some people are smarter or better than others. A fundamental tenet, flowing from this and found almost universally in our industrial status system, has been that workers and managers are engaged in different productive functions because they are actually different kinds of people. The manager is active. He plans, thinks, organizes, supervises, and controls work and likes doing so. The worker is passive. He is supervised and controlled, and that supervision is what he wants or likes. In other words, managers are proactive, workers only reactive. With rare exceptions, the literature and management itself is primarily concerned with the question: "If management does such and such, can we thereby get the worker to react in a certain desirable way?" Even Rensis Likert, with all his valid insistence on the worker as human being, is still operating within a framework in which managers are "high-producing" insofar as they act in such a way as to elicit certain *reactions* from others. It is at least arguable that the extent to which a worker's potential is not realized may not be due to any innate difference, but rather to a lack of opportunity in his environment, in his work environment no less than in his cultural, educational, or emotional environment. Finally, we suggest that the influences which make the manager active, creative, and absorbed in his work would produce the same effects in workers were they available to them.

It is important to note here, however, that this point of view is not simply another kind of manipulation of the worker. We would not propose that workers be given more control, more opportunity to be creative, more variety of activity in their jobs as a *means* to making the worker more productive or more satisfied, but rather as a right which all men should have. Our point is that whatever the future may hold, work has absorbed for a long time and still does the central part of a man's life. All other activities are secondary to it and must be organized around it. Most waking hours are spent either working, travelling to and from work, or preparing for work. A man finds his identity, his status, and his self-esteem through his work, not to mention his livelihood, his style of life, and many of his social relationships. He has a right then to expect that his work will provide him with the opportunity to be a fully functioning human being, where he can use and develop his talents and capacities as fully as possible and know that he makes an important contribution through the work that he does. It is enough. Why then should he need palliatives, personnel policies which trick him into *feeling* that he is important? Only because the basic underlying beliefs of management are that the jobs that workers do are boring, repetitious, uncreative, and unworthy, that it is inevitable that most people do such work and, consequently, that the worker must be lulled into a false sense of importance, or pushed and controlled through supervision. The worker is asked to adopt a security-seeking, passive role rather than an active, creative one —a choice which would be seen at once, if proposed for managers, as leading to stagnation.

The traditional view of the worker, that people hate work, that they must be coerced into working and controlled, and that they prefer matters this way because it enables them to avoid responsibility and gain security, was called by McGregor Theory X. He points out that application of this theory does not work effectively once workers have satisfied their basic physical needs (using Maslow's hierarchy of needs theory [see p. 52]). This view of the worker and management methods based on it were suited to the capabilities and characteristics of the child, but not of the adult. McGregor concludes, "so long as the assumptions of Theory X continue to influence managerial strategy, we will fail to discover, let alone utilize, the potentialities of the average human being."[3]

Likert cites the results of various studies of supervisory practices of high- and low-producing managers as empirical evidence of McGregor's philosophy.

> The common assumption that non-supervisory employees, given increased freedom, will loaf and not produce does not seem to be borne out by the evidence. . . . Managers who achieve high performance in their units accompanied by a sense of freedom supervise by setting general goals and objectives and providing less specific direction than do managers of low-producing units. . . . They use more participation and achieve higher involvement, greater interest in the work, and more responsibility for it than do the low-producing managers.[4]

In fact, McGregor's argument was the forerunner of the management philosophy, based on and supported by social scientific evidence, which has emerged in the 1960s.

Miller and Form have traced the changing definition of the worker since 1900.[5] At that time, the worker was considered a biological machine, and the problem of management was how to convert his energy to useful work. Since the worker's primary interest was believed to be money, the result was "scientific management" which introduced time and motion studies, and such incentive systems as piece rates, and work simplification (assembly line). Physical environmental conditions were studied to reduce distractions and discomfort .

The next view, said to have arisen in the 1920s, was that of the industrial psychologists. They believed that it was more important to understand that the individual differences between workers was greater than their similarities, that the worker was motivated, not rationally, but by individual needs such as advancement and recognition. This view gave rise to aptitude tests, and to efforts to fit the man to the job and to improve job satisfaction.

Stimulated largely by the findings of the Hawthorne Electric studies, the era beginning in 1940 discovered the importance of the work group and began to view the worker as a social man, to whom group life and membership were the most important motivators. The new techniques of management, developed to increase productivity and influenced by this philosophy, included group participation in decision-making, human relations training for managers, and the elaborate machinery of labour relations.

According to Miller and Form, the managerial philosophy now emerging could be called the "worker as a socio-political man" and assumes that the worker desires an active part in decisions which affect him at work and in the community. The result has been the introduction of staff meetings, T groups, the union as a communication and bargaining channel, profit-sharing programs, and other cooperative management plans.

It is important to notice that each philosophy arose as the result of new knowledge and the social necessities of the time. As McGregor points out, what is functional at one time is not necessarily functional under other circumstances. It is equally important to notice that each of these philosophies makes the assumption that managers are proactive and workers are reactive. Efficiency, creativity, and high morale are seen as the result, not of a universal human desire to achieve these things, but of management techniques intended to produce certain behaviour or reactions in workers. This contradiction between these worker demands for a serious adult status and management's tendency to see workers as irresponsible and reactive must be resolved if progress is to be made in labour relations. Work must be enriched and freed, and the worker must be more deeply involved in and satisfied with his work.

The most widely acclaimed method of achieving this optimum involvement is called "worker participation," which implies various degrees of worker involvement in decision-making in matters concerned with the work of industrial plants. The number of social scientific studies of such experiments is too great to go into here, but an excellent summary can be found in Blumberg's *Industrial Democracy: The Sociology of Participation*, chapters 5 and 6. Here it suffices to quote Blumberg's own summary. "There is hardly a study in the entire literature [of participation] which fails to demonstrate that satisfaction in work is enhanced or that other generally acknowledged beneficial consequences accrue from a genuine increase in workers' decision-making power. Such consistency of findings, I submit, is rare in social research."[6]

Such an experiment is currently being tried at the Alcan plant in Kingston, Canada. Time clocks have been eliminated, workers are on a weekly salary, and a general pattern of worker consultation on method of production with less and less supervision is already in effect. Both management and workers find the results rewarding and exciting.[7]

One factor stressed most strongly by both union and management leaders at Kingston is that their system is working only because there has been for some years an atmosphere of mutual trust and confidence between workers and management. They also emphasize that a training program of nearly two years' duration, established first for middle and lower management and later for workers, had prepared the way for unreserved acceptance of the philosophy behind worker participation. Their greatest problem was, actually, with the lower levels of supervisory staff, who were, of course, the most threatened by loss of authority. The point is made by all who have studied or been involved in such experiments: unless the principle is accepted by all levels of management, that management has much to gain and learn from sharing decision-making with the men who do the work, the effort will be sabotaged, intentionally or unintentionally.[8]

Our study suggests that perhaps one of the best reasons a manager can give himself for adopting such policies is that the workers will no longer, given their experiences and education, accept a system of distribution of power and status based on traditional definitions. In other words, the manager's right to control the conditions of work and to make decisions without consultation will no longer be accepted, and there are no longer any real distinctions in his education, life style, or work that can legitimate his right to exclusive control. In short, he would do well to read the handwriting on the wall, and, to mix metaphors, to quit while he is ahead.

Many forms of increased worker participation in decision-making are implicit in new managerial ideologies and strategies, such as goal-directed management and the Scanlon plan. This plan consists of a wage formula and a suggestion system. The wage formula increases wages (including

white collar and managerial) in direct proportion to increases in productivity, so that, for example, for every one per cent increase in productivity
there is a one per cent increase in wages. The suggestion system is one
in which proposals of the employees are processed by a departmental
suggestion committee made up of the foreman and union representatives.
If they apply to the whole plant, they go to a plant-wide committee.
Since these suggestions may result in profits which are shared by all
workers, they are encouraged to cooperate in making them. Workers are
regularly informed of the progress of their suggestions and, if at any
point they are rejected, they are told the reasons for the rejection. Evidently, this system results in greatly increased productivity (often as
much as 40 per cent) and in a deeper involvement of the workers with
the objectives of the plant (the number of useful suggestions sometimes
increases as much as 600 per cent).[9] Managerial innovations like the
Scanlon plan and other systems have been introduced in many European
countries, notably Germany, Holland, and Yugoslavia, with the same
results of increased worker participation. Furthermore, European unions
are now making worker participation a major issue at the bargain table.

These developments reflect adaptations being made to the emerging
worker. If they continue to spread and develop, the worker will enter a
new stage in his relationship to his work, one in which he can contribute
deeply of himself, can see his own ideas have an impact on the work,
and can find an outlet for his creativity. If he contributes, it will give him
a sense of his rights as a citizen, and of involvement in and satisfaction
from his society. It will encourage him to develop to the full his own
potentialities, to realize the possibilities of his own life.

With these developments, the emerging worker will gain a new and
more satisfying place in his society, and the world of work itself will be
renewed. Out of our pain and peril, we may produce a new life.

Notes

NOTES TO CHAPTER 1

1. *Canada Yearbook* (Ottawa: Queen's Printer, 1965), pp. 164–66.
2. C. P. Kindleberger, *Economic Development.*
3. Jean Fourastié, *The Causes of Wealth*, p. 103.
4. Ibid., p. 115.
5. Economic Council of Canada, "The Challenge of Growth and Change," *Fifth Annual Review*, September, 1968.
6. U.S. Department of Commerce, Current Population Reports, *Consumer Income*, Series P-60, no. 66, December 23, 1969; Washington, D.C.: U.S. Government Printing Office, 1969.
7. Nariman K. Dhalla, *These Canadians*, pp. 268, 419, 447.
8. United Nations, *Statistical Yearbook*, 1968, p. 586.
9. U.S. Department of Commerce, *Consumer Income*, p. 1.
10. Fourastié, *The Causes of Wealth*, pp. 123–24.
11. W. W. Rostow, *The Stages of Economic Growth*, pp. 4–10.
12. Ibid., p. 38.
13. Ibid., p. 59.
14. Ibid., pp. 10–11.
15. Dhalla, *These Canadians*, pp. 22, 29.
16. U.S. Department of Commerce, *Consumer Income*, p. 1, table A.
17. Kindleberger, *Economic Development*, pp. 113–15.

NOTES TO CHAPTER 2

1. George Katona, *The Mass Consumption Society*, p. 21.
2. Ibid., pp. 300 ff.

3. Sylvia Ostry, "The Female Worker: Labour Force and Occupational Trends," in *Changing Patterns in Women's Employment*, pp. 6, 9.

4. Ibid., p. 15.

5. Ibid., p. 19.

6. Ibid., p. 23.

7. D. A. Porter, *Report of the Royal Commission on Banking and Finance*, pp. 15–16.

8. Survey Research Center, *Survey of Consumer Finances*, Ann Arbor: University of Michigan, 1963.

9. Porter, *Banking and Finance*. All findings reported here are found in chapter 2, "Personal Finance," pp. 13–31.

10. The information in this section is drawn from unpublished DBS tables prepared especially for this paper.

11. DBS, *Family Income and Expenditure in Canada, 1937–38* (Ottawa: King's Printer, 1941), p. 182.

12. D. Reisman and H. Roseborough, "Careers and Consumer Behaviour," in *Abundance for What?*, ed. D. Reisman (New York: Doubleday, 1964), pp. 107–30.

13. Reuel Denney, "The Leisure Society," p. 49.

14. Ibid.

15. Ferdynand Zweig, *The Worker in an Affluent Society*, p. 135.

16. D. Reisman, "Leisure and Work in Postindustrial Society," in *Abundance for What?*, ed. D. Reisman, p. 170.

17. Katona, *The Mass Consumption Society*, p. 275.

18. Zweig, *The Worker in an Affluent Society*, p. 71.

19. Charles E. Silberman, "The Drift to Early Retirement," *Fortune* 71, no. 5 (May, 1965): 113 ff.

20. A. Hecksher and Sebastian de Grazia, "Problems in Review," pp. 133–34.

21. D. Pécaut, "The Worker and the Community," in *Workers' Attitudes to Technical Change*, ed. A. Touraine et al. (Paris: OECD, 1965), pp 133–34.

22. John K. Galbraith, *The Affluent Society*, pp. 95–96.

23. C. P. Kindleberger, *Economic Development*, p. 35 and chapter 8, 2nd ed.

NOTES TO CHAPTER 3

1. Jean Fourastié, *The Causes of Wealth*, p. 176.

2. DBS Bulletin, 7.1–10, *Educational Levels and School Attendance*, 1961, pp. 10–15.

3. DBS Bulletin Cat. 71–505, *Educational Attainment of the Canadian Population and Labour Force: 1960–65*.

4. W. M. Illing and Z. E. Zsigmond, *Enrolment in Schools and Universities, 1951–52 to 1975–76*, Economic Council of Canada, Staff Study no. 20, October (Ottawa: Queen's Printer, 1967), p. 28.

5. OECD, *Development of Secondary Education, Trends and Implications* (Paris: 1969), p. 32.

6. Illing and Zsigmond, *Enrolment in Schools and Universities*, p. 28.

7. Fourastié, *The Causes of Wealth*, p. 175.

8. Noah M. Meltz, *Changes in the Occupational Composition of the Canadian Labour Force*, p. 65.

9. Canada, Department of Labour, *Acquisition of Skills*, pp. 17–18.

10. Ibid.

11. Meltz, *Changes in Labour Force*, p. 61.

12. Edward F. Denison, *The Source of Economic Growth in the United States and the Alternatives Before Us*, p. 269.

13. Gordon Bertram, *The Contribution of Education to Economic Growth*, pp. 55–56.

14. Nalla Gouden, "Investment in Education in India," *Journal of Human Resources* 2, no. 3 (Summer, 1967): 352.

15. Canada, Department of Labour, *Skilled and Professional Manpower in Canada, 1945–65*, p. 103.

16. Ibid., p. 34.

17. Bertram, *Contribution of Education*, p. 146.

18. S. M. Miller, "The Outlook of Working-Class Youth," in *Blue Collar World*, ed. A. B. Shostak and W. Gomberg (Englewood Cliffs, N.J.: Prentice-Hall, 1964), pp. 124–25.

19. Denison, Appendix to "Measuring the Contribution of Education to Economic Growth," in *The Residual Factor and Economic Growth* (Paris: OECD, 1965), pp. 13–94.

20. Miller, "Working-Class Youth," pp. 124–25.

21. Bertram, *Contribution of Education*, p. 59.

22. Stephen G. Peitchinis, *The Economics of Labour, Employment and Wages in Canada*, p. 23.

23. Richard Centers, "Educational and Occupational Mobility," p. 144.

24. Gladys Palmer, *Labor Mobility in Six Cities*, p. 134.

25. S. M. Lipset and R. Bendix, *Social Mobility in Industrial Society*, p. 92.

26. Lloyd G. Reynolds, *The Structure of Labor Markets, Wages and Labor Mobility in Theory and Practice*, p. 24.

27. *Steel Workers and Technical Progress*, E. P. A. Project no. 164, Industrial Version, no. 2, pp. 22, 31.

28. Grant Venn, *Man, Education and Work*, p. 98.

29. Lipset and Bendix, *Social Mobility*, p. 91.

30. T. Purcell, *Blue Collar Man*, Cambridge, Mass., Harvard University Press, 1960.

31. Eli Chinoy, *Automobile Workers and the American Dream*.

32. B. M. Berger, *Working Class Suburb*, pp. 20–21.

33. Gérald Fortin and Louis-Marie Tremblay, "Attitudes à l'égard des occupations dans une paroisse agricole," p. 37.

34. J. Dofny and Hélène David, "Les aspirations des travailleurs de la métallurgie," pp. 68, 83.

35. F. W. Rowe, "People Who Want to Move," *Atlantic Advocate* 58, no. 2 (October, 1967): 74.

36. Marc Abrams, *Education, Social Class and Reading of Newspapers and Magazines*, London: Institute of Practitioners in Advertising, January, 1966.

37. Sebastian de Grazia, *Of Time, Work and Leisure*, p. 462.

38. Alex Inkeles, "Industrial Man," p. 25.

39. Dofny and David, "Aspirations des travailleurs," pp. 66–67.

40. Peter Drucker, "Is Business Letting Young People Down?," *Harvard Business Review* 43, no. 6 (November–December, 1965): 51.

41. Lee Danielson, *Characteristics of Engineers and Scientists* (Ann Arbor: University of Michigan, Bureau of Industrial Relations, 1960), p. 68.

42. A. Kornhauser, *Mental Health of the Industrial Worker*, p. 137.

43. G. A. Almond and Sidney Verba, *The Civic Culture*, pp. 380–81.

44. Harold L. Wilensky, *Intellectuals in Labour Unions*, pp. 266–67.

45. Ibid., p. 267.

46. Gad Horowitz, *Canadian Labour in Politics*, p. 150.

47. Robert Alford, *Party and Society*, p. 333.

48. Ibid., pp. 352–54.

49. Horowitz, *Canadian Labour in Politics*, p. 41.

50. V. L. Allen, *Militant Trade Unionism*, p. 105.

NOTES TO CHAPTER 4

1. Charles E. Silberman, "The Real News about Automation," *Fortune* 71, no. 1 (January, 1965): 124 ff.
2. Ibid., p. 222.
3. James R. Bright, *Automation and Management*, pp. 170–211.
4. Ibid., p. 205.
5. Jiri Nehnevajsu, "Automation and Social Stratification," p. 404.
6. Silberman, "News about Automation," pp. 113 ff.
7. W. H. Scott et al., *Men, Steel and Technical Change*, p. 29; Charles Walker, *Toward the Automated Factory*, p. 60; and Floyd C. Mann, "Psychological and Organizational Impacts," in *Automation and Technological Change*, ed. J. T. Dunlop, The American Assembly (New York: Columbia University Press, 1962), p. 53.
8. Mann, "Psychological and Organizational Impacts," p. 53.
9. Scott, *Men, Steel and Technical Change*, p. 12.
10. Ibid., p. 13.
11. C. Durand, "Conséquences de la modernisation sur l'évolution des relations de travail," pp. 177–92.
12. Scott, *Men, Steel and Technical Change*, p. 23.
13. Walker, *Toward the Automated Factory*.
14. Bright, *Automation and Management*, p. 201.
15. Walker, *Toward the Automated Factory*, p. 60.
16. Durand, "Conséquences de la modernisation," pp. 184–86.
17. *Steel Workers and Technical Progress*, E. P. A. Project no. 164, Industrial Version no. 2, pp. 22–23.
18. P. Dubin, "Industrial Workers' Worlds," pp. 131–42.
19. J. Goldthorpe et al., *The Affluent Worker: Industrial Attitudes and Behaviour*, p. 53.
20. Dubin, "Industrial Workers' Worlds," pp. 140–41.
21. Goldthorpe, *Industrial Attitudes*, pp. 63–68.
22. P. Naville, *Vers l'automatisme social?*, p. 192.
23. A. H. Maslow, *Motivation and Personality* (New York: Harper & Bros., 1954), pp. 80–106.
24. Goldthorpe, *Industrial Attitudes*, chapter 2.
25. A. Kornhauser, *Mental Health of the Industrial Worker*, pp. 205–7.
26. R. Blauner, *Alienation and Freedom*, pp. 183–84.
27. A. Sturmthal, ed., *White Collar Unionism*, p. 367.
28. C. Wright Mills, *White Collar*, p. 212.
29. D. Lockwood, *The Blackcoated Worker* (London: George Allen and Unwin, 1958), pp. 78–79, 85.
30. Sylvia Ostry, "The Female Worker in Canada," in *Changing Patterns in Women's Employment*, p. 44.
31. Mills, *White Collar*, p. 198.
32. Sturmthal, *White Collar Unionism*, p. 395.
33. Peter F. Drucker, *Landmarks of Tomorrow*, p. 62.
34. Ida Moos, "The Computer Takes Over the Office," p. 109.
35. Goldthorpe, *Industrial Attitudes*, p. 129.

NOTES TO CHAPTER 5

1. Noah M. Meltz, *Changes in the Occupational Composition of the Canadian Labour Force*, pp. 26–33.
2. Charles E. Silberman, "What Hit the Teenagers?," *Fortune* 71, no. 4 (April,

1965): 130 ff., and "The Drift to Early Retirement," *Fortune* 71, no. 4 (April, 1965): 113 ff.

3. Meltz, *Changes in Canadian Labour Force*, pp. 26–27 and table 4.

4. Peter F. Drucker, *Landmarks of Tomorrow*, p. 100.

5. N. Foote and Paul Hatt, "Social Mobility and Economic Advancement," pp. 364–78.

6. M. Berman, "Vertical Mobility," in *The Reluctant Job Changer*, ed. Gladys Palmer (Philadelphia: University of Pennsylvania Press, 1962), p. 151; and S. M. Lipset and R. Bendix, *Social Mobility in Industrial Society*, pp. 12–13.

7. Lipset and Bendix, *Social Mobility*, p. 88.

8. Yves de Jocas and Guy Rocher, "Inter-Generation Occupational Mobility in the Province of Quebec," in *Canadian Society*, ed. B. Blishen et al. (Toronto: Macmillan Company of Canada, 1964), pp. 445–46.

9. John Porter, *The Vertical Mosaic*, p. 93.

10. R. Dubin, *The World of Work: Industrial Society and Human Relations*, pp. 270–71, and table 15.4.

11. Lloyd G. Reynolds, *Structure of Labor Markets, Wages and Labor Mobility in Theory and Practice*, p. 152.

12. Ibid., p. 153.

13. J. Dofny and Hélène David, "Les aspirations des travailleurs," p. 70.

14. A. Sturmthal, ed., *White Collar Unionism*, p. 396.

15. Gladys Palmer, *Labor Mobility in Six Cities*, pp. 121–38.

16. Ibid., p. 124; and Reynolds, *Labor Markets*, p. 40.

17. DBS, "Labour Mobility of Persons Covered by Unemployment Insurance," *Canadian Statistical Review*, November, 1961, p. iii, table 3.

18. Stephen G. Peitchinis, *The Economics of Labour, Employment and Wages in Canada*, p. 13.

19. Palmer, *Labor Mobility*, pp. 121–38; and Reynolds, *Labor Markets*, p. 40.

20. G. Barbichon, *Adaptation and Training of Rural Workers for Industrial Work*.

21. D. Pécaut, "Worker in Community," in *Workers' Attitudes to Technical Change*, ed. A. Touraine et al. (Paris: OECD, 1965).

22. *Steel Workers and Technical Progress*, E. P. A. Project no. 164, Industrial Version, no. 3, p. 47.

23. Palmer, *Labor Mobility*, p. 73.

24. "The People in the U.S.A.—A Self-Portrait," *Fortune* 21, February, 1940, pp. 14 ff.

25. George Katona, *The Mass Consumption Society*, pp. 107–9.

26. Lipset and Bendix, *Social Mobility*, pp. 77–78.

27. Talcott Parsons, "An Analytical Approach to the Theory of Social Stratification," *American Journal of Sociology* 45, no. 6 (1940): 841–62.

28. Lipset, "Value Differences, Absolute or Relative: The English Speaking Democracies," in *Canadian Society*, ed. Blishen et al., pp. 325–40.

29. Kaspar Naegele, "Canadian Society: Further Reflections," in *Canadian Society*, ed. Blishen et al., p. 501.

30. Lipset, "Value Differences," p. 335.

31. Porter, *The Vertical Mosaic*, pp. 54–55.

32. Ibid., p. 54.

33. Canada, Department of Labour, *Acquisition of Skills*, p. 10.

34. Ibid., p. 17.

35. Canada, Department of Labour, *Skilled and Professional Manpower in Canada*.

36. Porter, *The Vertical Mosaic*, pp. 48–49.

37. S. M. Miller, "Comparative Social Mobility," *Current Sociology* 9, no. 1 (1960): 36.

38. Lipset and Bendix, *Social Mobility*, p. 74.
39. Robert Alford, *Party and Society*, p. 118; and Miller, "Comparative Social Mobility," p. 35.
40. Lipset, "Value Differences," p. 336.
41. Ibid., p. 340, fn. 47.
42. John Crispo, *International Unionism*, pp. 245–47.
43. As quoted in Lipset, "Value Differences," p. 160.
44. Lipset and Bendix, "Social Mobility and Occupational Career Patterns, II, Social Mobility," *American Journal of Sociology* 57 (March, 1952): 502–3.
45. Dofny and David, "Les aspirations des travailleurs," p. 73.
46. Jean Fourastié, *The Causes of Wealth*, p. 229.
47. Foote and Hatt, "Social Mobility and Economic Advancement," pp. 366–67. Italics are ours.

NOTES TO CHAPTER 6

1. R. F. Hamilton, "The Behavior and Values of Skilled Workers," in *Blue Collar World*, ed. A. B. Shostak and W. Gomberg, pp. 55–56.
2. W. M. Dobriner, *Class in Suburbia*, Englewood Cliffs, N.J.: Prentice-Hall (1963): 49–60.
3. S. D. Clark, *The Suburban Society*, ch. 4.
4. Eli Chinoy, *Automobile Workers and the American Dream*, p. xv.
5. W. F. Whyte, *Industry and Society*, pp. 88–89.
6. P. E. Pineo, "The Extended Family in a Working-Class Area of Hamilton," in *Canadian Society*, ed. B. Blishen et al., pp. 135 ff.; and P. Garigue, "French Canadian Kinship and Urban Life," *American Anthropologist* 57, no. 6 (December, 1956): 1090 ff.
7. B. Berger, *Working Class Suburb*, p. 22.
8. Chinoy, *Automobile Workers*, p. 126.
9. Ferdynand Zweig, *The Worker in an Affluent Society*, p. 128.
10. Ibid., p. 6.
11. M. M. Gordon and C. H. Anderson, "The Blue-Collar Worker at Leisure," in *Blue Collar World*, ed. A. B. Shostak and W. Gomberg, p. 413.
12. Ibid., p. 412.
13. Clark, *The Suburban Society*, p. 172.
14. Ibid., p. 173.
15. Berger, *Working Class Suburb*, p. 71.
16. N. Hurvitz, "Marital Strains in the Blue Collar Family," in *Blue Collar World*, ed. A. B. Shostak and W. Gomberg, p. 95.
17. Zweig, *Worker in an Affluent Society*, p. 5.
18. Berger, *Working Class Suburb*, p. 64.
19. Zweig, *Worker in an Affluent Society*, p. 134.
20. A. E. Barkan, "The Union Member: Profile and Attitudes," *American Federationist* 74, no. 8 (August, 1967), 1 ff.
21. Berger, *Working Class Suburb*, pp. 32–39.
22. J. H. Goldthorpe et al., "The Affluent Worker and the Thesis of Embourgeoisement," *Sociology* 1, no. 1 (January, 1967): 24.
23. Goldthorpe et al., *The Affluent Worker: Political Attitudes*, pp. 57–58.
24. P. C. Sexton, "Wife of the Happy Worker," in *Blue Collar World*, ed. A. B. Shostak and W. Gomberg, p. 82.
25. Ibid., p. 82.
26. L. Rainwater, R. P. Coleman, and G. Handel, *Workingman's Wife: Her Personality, World and Life Style*, pp. 70 ff.
27. Sexton, "Wife of the Happy Worker," p. 84.

28. Ben H. Bagdikian, *In the Midst of Plenty*, p. 53.

29. M. Schwartz and G. Henderson, "The Culture of Unemployment: Some Notes on Negro Children," in *Blue Collar World*, ed. A. B. Shostak and W. Gomberg, p. 474.

30. Bagdikian, *In the Midst of Plenty*, p. 45.

31. Ibid., p. 73.

32. Ibid., p. 68.

33. Zweig, *Worker in Affluent Society*, pp. 23 ff.

34. Ibid., p. 180.

35. L. Rainwater and G. Handel, "Changing Family Roles in the Working Class," in *Blue Collar World*, ed. A. B. Shostak and W. Gomberg, p. 73.

36. Mirra Komarovsky, *Blue Collar Marriage*, pp. 320–22.

37. Paraphrase of statement contained in Hurvitz, "Marital Status," p. 108.

38. Ibid., p. 100.

39. Rainwater and Handel, "Changing Family Roles," p. 74.

40. M. Adélard Tremblay, "Les tensions psychologiques chez le bucheron; quelques éléments d'explication," p. 74.

41. Chinoy, *Automobile Workers*, p. 127.

42. Tremblay, "Les tensions psychologiques," pp. 77–78.

43. Zweig, *Worker in an Affluent Society*, p. 207.

44. T. Purcell, *Blue Collar Man* (Cambridge, Mass.: Harvard University Press, 1960), p. 161.

45. W. G. Dyer, "Family Reactions to the Father's Job," in *Blue Collar World*, ed. A. B. Shostak and W. Gomberg, p. 86.

46. R. Guest, "Work Careers and Aspirations of Mass Production Workers," p. 162.

47. Charles Walker, *Toward the Automatic Factory*, p. 200.

48. Guest, "Work Careers and Aspirations," p. 162.

49. James R. Bright, *Automation and Management*, p. 201.

50. Ibid., p. 201.

51. Ibid., p. 200.

52. Walker, *Toward the Automatic Factory*, p. 83.

53. Ibid., p. 83.

54. Ibid., p. xix.

55. Ibid., p. 50.

56. Ibid., p. 75.

57. A. Hecksher and Sebastian de Grazia, "Problems in Review," p. 8.

58. Ida Moos, "When the Computer Takes Over the Office," p. 105.

59. Manuscript by Jennifer MacLaughlin.

60. E. M. Kassalow, "White-Collar Unionism in the United States," in *White Collar Unionism*, ed. A. Sturmthal, p. 358.

61. Ibid., p. 359.

NOTES TO CHAPTER 7

1. British figures: "Trade Unions in Britain," London: British Information Services, RF. P. 5682/69 (January, 1969), p. 3; U.S. figures: Department of Labor, Bureau of Labor Statistics, "Directory of National and International Labor Unions in the United States," 1967 (Bulletin No. 1596).

2. W. H. Miernyk, *Trade Unions in the Age of Affluence*, p. 149.

3. Ibid., p. 107.

4. A. H. Raskin, "The Squeeze on Unions," in *Labor and the National Economy*, ed. W. G. Bowen (New York: W. H. Norton & Co., 1965), pp. 4–5.

5. Ben B. Seligman, *Most Notorious Victory*, pp. 240–51.

6. E. Dumas-Gagnon, "Le conflit provoqué par Walter Reuther," *Le Devoir,* June 14, 1967, p. 5.

7. Charles Levinson, *Collective Bargaining in Perspective,* Report IB, OECD, Manpower and Social Affairs Directorate, Paris: November, 1969, p. 14.

8. "Labour, More of the Same?," *Monetary Times,* January, 1967, pp. 48–50.

9. Quoted in the *Labour Gazette* 67, no. 10 (October, 1967): 624 ff.

10. Canada, Department of Labour, *Labour Gazette* 67, no. 2 (February, 1967): 94; and *Labour Gazette* 68, no. 2 (February, 1968): 91–95.

11. See Wilensky, *Intellectuals in Labour Unions,* ch. 13.

12. Alex Inkeles, *The Modernization of Man,* p. 147.

13. A. Sturmthal, ed., *White Collar Unionism,* p. 375.

14. Ibid., p. 375.

15. Ibid., p. 389.

16. Quoted in ibid., p. 201.

17. Levinson, "Collective Bargaining," p. 14.

18. For a good discussion of management's approach, see Miernyk, *Trade Unions in the Age of Affluence,* pp. 106–23.

19. S. Wallen, "How Issues of Subcontracting and Plant Removal are Handled by Arbitrators," *Industrial and Labour Relations Review* 19, no. 2 (January, 1966), as quoted in D. E. Cullen and M. L. Greenbaum, "Management Rights and Collective Bargaining: Can Both Survive?," p. 59.

20. N. Foote, "The Professionalization of Labor in Detroit," pp. 371–80.

21. Ibid., p. 373.

22. C. Jodoin, "Management Rights in an Era of Technological Change," *Canadian Labour* 11, no. 4 (April, 1966): 21.

23. C. Durand, "Reintegration of Work Tasks," in *Workers' Attitudes to Technical Change,* ed. A. Touraine et al. (Paris: OECD, 1965), p. 47.

24. S. Jamieson, *Industrial Relations in Canada,* p. 124.

25. As quoted in *McGill Industrial Relations Centre Review* 1, no. 1 (Winter, 1966–67): 4.

26. J. T. Dunlop, "The Social Utility of Collective Bargaining," in *Challenges to Collective Bargaining,* ed. Lloyd Ulman (Englewood Cliffs, N.J.: Prentice-Hall, 1967), p. 168.

27. R. L. Raimon, *Affluence, Collective Bargaining and Steel,* pp. 980–85.

28. Jean-Réal Cardin, "Manpower Adjustment to Technological Change and Labour Relations in Canada," p. 54.

NOTES TO CHAPTER 8

1. Robert Dreeban, *On What is Learned in School,* Reading, Mass., Addison-Wesley, 1968.

2. Peter F. Drucker, "The Employee Society," pp. 358–63.

3. R. K. Merton, *Social Theory and Social Structure* (Glencoe, Ill.: Free Press of Glencoe, 1957), ch. 4.

4. O. Hall and B. McFarlane, *Transition from School to Work.*

NOTES TO CHAPTER 9

1. W. F. Whyte, *Money and Motivation,* pp. 94–95.

2. Daniel Katz, "Satisfactions and Deprivations in Industrial Life," in *Industrial Conflict,* ed. A. Kornhauser et al. (New York: McGraw-Hill, 1954), p. 93.

3. Douglas McGregor, *The Human Side of Management,* p. 42.

4. Rensis Likert, *New Patterns of Management*, pp. 20–21.

5. D. C. Miller and W. H. Form, *Industrial Sociology*, pp. 643–86.

6. Paul Blumberg, *Industrial Democracy*, p. 123.

7. "Industrial Innovation at Kingston Plant of ALCAN," *McGill Industrial Relations Review*, Fall, 1969, p. 3.

8. Ibid.

9. George Shultz and Robert Crisera, "The Lapointe Machine Tool Co., and the United Steelworkers of America," *Causes of Industrial Peace under Collective Bargaining*, Case Study no. 10, Washington, D.C.: National Planning Association (1952): 55.

A Selected
Bibliography

I. BOOKS AND PAMPHLETS

Alford, Robert. *Party and Society: The Anglo-American Democracies.* Chicago: Rand McNally, 1963.

Allen, V. L. *Militant Trade Unionism.* London: The Merlin Press, 1966.

Almond, G. A., and Verba, Sidney. *The Civic Culture: Political Attitudes and Democracy in Five Nations.* Princeton, N.J.: Princeton University Press, 1963.

Bagdikian, Ben H. *In the Midst of Plenty: A New Report on the Poor in America.* Boston: Signet Books, 1964.

Barbichon, G. *Adaptation and Training of Rural Workers for Industrial Work.* Paris: OECD, 1962.

Bell, D. *The End of Ideology.* Glencoe, Ill.: Free Press of Glencoe, 1960.

Berger, B. *Working Class Suburb: A Study of Auto Workers in Suburbia.* Berkeley: University of California Press, 1960.

Bertram, Gordon. *The Contribution of Education to Economic Growth.* Economic Council of Canada, Occasional Paper no. 12. Ottawa: Queen's Printer, 1966.

Blauner, R. *Alienation and Freedom.* Chicago: University of Chicago Press, 1964.

Blishen, B. R.; Jones, F. E.; Naegele, K. D.; and Porter, John. *Canadian Society: Sociological Perspectives.* Toronto: Macmillan Company of Canada, 1964.

Blumberg, Paul. *Industrial Democracy: The Sociology of Participation.* New York: Schocken Books, 1969.

Bright, James R. *Automation and Management.* Division of Research, Graduate School of Business Administration, Harvard University. Cambridge, Mass.: Plimpton Press, 1958.

Canada, Department of Labour. *Acquisition of Skills*. Research Program on the Training of Skilled Manpower no. 4. Ottawa: Queen's Printer, April, 1960.
————. *Married Women Working for Pay in Eight Canadian Cities*. Ottawa: Queen's Printer, 1958.
————. *Skilled and Professional Manpower in Canada, 1945–65*. Royal Commission on Canada's Economic Prospects. Ottawa: Queen's Printer, 1957.
Canada, Senate Committee on Manpower and Employment. *Electrical and Electronics Industry and Heavy Machinery Industry*. Technological Change and Skilled Manpower. Ottawa: Queen's Printer, 1957.
————. *The Household Appliance Industry*. Technological Change and Skilled Manpower. Ottawa: Queen's Printer, 1958.
————. *The Automobile and Parts Manufacturing Industries*. Technological Change and Skilled Manpower. Ottawa: Queen's Printer, 1960.
————. *Electronic Data Processing Occupations in a Large Insurance Company*. Technological Change and Skilled Manpower. Ottawa: Queen's Printer, 1961.
————. *Technological Changes and Their Impact on Employment and Occupations*. Technological Change and Skilled Manpower. Ottawa: Queen's Printer, 1961.
Cardin, Jean-Réal. "Manpower Adjustment to Technological Change and Labour Relations in Canada." Economic Council of Canada, National Conference on Labour-Management Relations. Mimeographed report. Montreal, November 21–22, 1966.
Chernik, S. E. *Interregional Disparities in Income*. Economic Council of Canada, Staff Study no. 14. Ottawa: Queen's Printer, August, 1966.
Chinoy, Eli. *Automobile Workers and the American Dream*. Garden City, N.Y.: Doubleday & Co., 1955.
Clarke, S. D. *The Suburban Society*. Toronto: University of Toronto Press, 1966.
Clements, R. V. *Managers: A Study of Their Careers in Industry*. London: Allen & Unwin, 1958.
Copeman, G. H. *Leaders of British Industry: A Study of the Careers of More Than a Thousand Public Company Directors*. London: Gee, 1955.
Corbett, David C. *Canada's Immigration Policy*. Toronto: University of Toronto Press, 1957.
Crispo, John. *International Unionism: A Study of Canadian-American Relations*. Toronto: McGraw-Hill, 1967.
Cullen, D. E., and Greenbaum, M. L. *Management Rights and Collective Bargaining: Can Both Survive?* Bulletin 58, New York State School of Industrial and Labor Relations. Ithaca, N.Y.: Cornell University Press, August, 1966.
De Grazia, Sebastian. *Of Time, Work and Leisure*. New York: The Twentieth Century Fund, 1962.
Denison, Edward F. *The Source of Economic Growth in the United States and the Alternatives Before Us*. Committee for Economic Development. Supplementary Paper no. 13. New York, 1962.
Denton, Frank T. *An Analysis of Interregional Differences in Manpower Utilization and Earnings*. Economic Council of Canada, Staff Study no. 15. Ottawa: Queen's Printer, April, 1966.
————; Kasahara, Yoshiko; and Ostry, Sylvia. *Population and Labour Force Projections to 1970*. Economic Council of Canada, Staff Study no. 1. Ottawa: Queen's Printer, 1964.
Dhalla, Nariman K. *These Canadians: A Sourcebook of Marketing and Socio-Economic Facts*. Toronto: McGraw-Hill, 1966.

Drucker, Peter F. *Landmarks of Tomorrow*. New York: Harper & Bros., 1959.

Dubin, R. *The World of Work: Industrial Society and Human Relations*. Englewood Cliffs, N.J.: Prentice-Hall, 1958.

Dunlop, J. T., ed. *Automation and Technological Change*. The American Assembly. New York: Columbia University Press, 1962.

Economic Council of Canada. *Annual Reviews*, nos. 4, 5, 6. Ottawa: Queen's Printer, 1967, 1968, 1969.

Fourastié, Jean. *The Causes of Wealth*. Translated by Theodore Caplow. Glencoe, Ill.: Free Press of Glencoe, 1960.

Galbraith, John K. *The Affluent Society*. Boston: Houghton Mifflin, 1958.

Goldthorpe, J. H.; Lockwood, D.; Bechhofer, F.; and Platt, J. *The Affluent Worker: Industrial Attitudes and Behaviour*. Cambridge, Mass.: Cambridge University Press, 1968.

———; Lockwood, D.; Bechhofer, F.; and Platt, J. *The Affluent Worker: Political Attitudes and Behaviour*. Cambridge, Mass.: Cambridge University Press, 1968.

Hall, O., and McFarlane, B. *Transition from School to Work*. Ottawa: Queen's Printer, 1962.

Horowitz, Gad. *Canadian Labour in Politics*. Toronto: University of Toronto Press, 1968.

Inkeles, Alex. *The Modernization of Man*. Reprint Series, The Center for International Affairs. Cambridge, Mass.: Harvard University Press, 1967.

Jamieson, S. *Industrial Relations in Canada*. Toronto: Macmillan Co. of Canada, 1957.

Kahl, Joseph. *The American Class Structure*. New York: Rinehart, 1957.

Katona, George. *The Mass Consumption Society*. New York: McGraw-Hill, 1964.

——— et al. *Survey of Consumer Finances*. Monographs 35–42, 1959–1965. Survey Research Center. Ann Arbor: University of Michigan.

Keniston, Kenneth. *Uncommitted Alienated Youth in American Society*. New York: Harcourt, Brace & World, 1965.

Kindleberger, C. P. *Economic Development*. 1st ed., 1958; 2nd ed., 1965. Toronto: McGraw-Hill.

Komarovsky, Mirra. *Blue Collar Marriage*. New York: Random House, 1964.

Kornhauser, A. *Mental Health of the Industrial Worker*. New York: John Wiley & Sons, 1965.

———; Dubin, R.; and Ross, A. M. *Industrial Conflict*. New York: McGraw-Hill, 1954.

Likert, Rensis. *New Patterns of Management*. New York, Toronto, London: McGraw-Hill, 1961.

Lipset, S. M., and Bendix, R. *Social Mobility in Industrial Society*. Berkeley: University of California Press, 1959.

Long, C. D. *The Labour Force under Changing Income and Employment*. Princeton, N.J.: Princeton University Press, 1958.

Mallett, Serge. *La nouvelle classe ouvrière*. Paris: Éditions du Seuil, 1963.

McGregor, Douglas. *The Human Side of Management*. New York: McGraw-Hill, 1960.

Meltz, Noah M. *Changes in the Occupational Composition of the Canadian Labour Force, 1931–61*. Economics and Research Branch, Department of

Labour, Canada, Occasional Paper no. 2. Ottawa: Queen's Printer, March, 1965.

Miernyk, W. H. *Trade Unions in the Age of Affluence.* New York: Random House, 1965.

Miller, D. C., and Form, W. H. *Industrial Sociology: A Sociology of Work Organizations.* 2nd ed. New York: Harper & Row, 1964.

Mills, C. Wright. *White Collar.* New York: Oxford University Press, 1951.

National Manpower Council. *Work in the Lives of Married Women.* Proceedings of a Conference on Womanpower, October 20–25, 1957. New York: Columbia University Press, 1958.

Naville, P. *Vers l'automatisme social?* Paris: Gallimard, 1963.

Nye, F. Ivan, and Hoffman, Louis Wladis. *The Employed Mother in America.* Chicago: Rand McNally & Co., 1963.

Organization for Economic Cooperation and Development. *The Residual Factor and Economic Growth.* Paris, 1964.

Ostry, Sylvia. *Changing Patterns in Women's Employment.* Canada, Department of Labour. Ottawa: Queen's Printer, 1966.

Palmer, Gladys. *Labor Mobility in Six Cities.* Social Science Research Council. New York, 1954.

———. *The Reluctant Job Changer.* Philadelphia: University of Pennsylvania Press, 1962.

Peitchinis, Stephen G. *The Economics of Labour, Employment and Wages in Canada.* Toronto: McGraw-Hill, 1965.

Porter, D. A. *Report of the Royal Commission on Banking and Finance.* Ottawa: Queen's Printer, 1964.

Porter, John. *The Vertical Mosaic.* Toronto: University of Toronto Press, 1965.

Raimon, R. L. *Affluence, Collective Bargaining and Steel.* Reprint Series no. 102, New York State School of Industrial Relations. Ithaca, N.Y.: Cornell University Press, 1960.

Rainwater, Lee; Coleman, Richard; and Handel, Gerald. *Workingman's Wife: Her Personality, World and Life Style.* Social Research Inc. New York: Oceana Publications Inc., 1959.

Reynolds, Lloyd G. *The Structure of Labor Markets, Wages and Labor Mobility in Theory and Practice.* New York: Harper & Bros., 1951.

Rogoff, N. *Recent Trends in Occupational Mobility.* Glencoe, Ill.: Free Press of Glencoe, 1953.

Rostow, W. W. *The Stages of Economic Growth.* Cambridge, England: Cambridge University Press, 1960.

Scott, W. H., and Banks, Olive. *Men, Steel and Technical Change.* Industrial Research Section, Department of Social Science, University of Liverpool. London, 1957.

Seligman, Ben B. *Most Notorious Victory: Man in an Age of Automation.* New York: The Free Press, 1966.

Shostak, Arthur B., and Gomberg, William, eds. *Blue Collar World: Studies of the American Worker.* Englewood Cliffs, N.J.: Prentice-Hall, 1964.

Steel Workers and Technical Progress. A Comparative Report on Six National Studies. E. P. A. Project no. 164, Industrial Version, nos. 2 and 3. Organization for European Economic Co-operation. Paris, June, 1959.

Sturmthal, A., ed. *White Collar Unionism.* Urbana and London: University of Illinois Press, 1966.

Taussig, F. N., and Jaslyn, C. S. *American Business Leaders.* New York: Macmillan Company, 1932.

Theobald, Robert. *The Rich and the Poor: A Study of the Economics of Rising Expectations.* New York: Mentor Books, 1961.

Touraine, A. et al. *Workers' Attitudes to Technical Change: Industrial Relations Aspects of Manpower Policy.* Paris: OECD, 1965.

Tremblay, M. A., and Fortin, G. *Les comportements économiques de la famille salariée de Québec.* Québec: Université Laval, 1964.

Ulman, Lloyd, ed. *Challenges to Collective Bargaining.* The American Assembly, Columbia University. Englewood Cliffs, N.J.: Prentice-Hall, 1967.

Venn, Grant. *Man, Education and Work.* American Council on Education. Washington, D.C., 1964.

Walker, Charles. *Toward the Automatic Factory.* New Haven: Yale University Press, 1957.

———, and Guest, Robert H. *The Man on the Assembly Line.* Cambridge, Mass.: Harvard University Press, 1952.

Warner, W. L., and Martin, N. H., eds. *Industrial Man: Businessmen and Business Organizations.* New York: Harper & Bros., 1959.

Whyte, W. F. *Industry and Society.* Toronto: McGraw-Hill, 1946.

———. *Money and Motivation.* New York: Harper & Bros., 1955.

Wilensky, Harold L. *Intellectuals in Labour Unions.* Glencoe, Ill.: Free Press of Glencoe, 1956.

Zweig, Ferdynand. *The Worker in an Affluent Society.* Toronto: Heinemann, 1961.

II. ARTICLES

Barbash, Jack. "Prospects for Future Growth: The Union Leadership Factor." *Proceedings of the Fifteenth Annual Meeting.* Industrial Relations Research Association. Pittsburgh, December 27–28, 1962.

Barken, A. E. "The Union Member: Profile and Attitudes." *American Federationist* 74, no. 8 (August, 1967): 1 ff.

Bell, Daniel. "The Great Back-to-Work Movement." Women and Business Series II, *Fortune* (July, 1956): 90–93.

Centers, Richard. "Education and Occupational Mobility." *American Sociological Review* 14, no. 1 (February, 1949): 143–44.

Denney, Reuel. "The Leisure Society." *Harvard Business Review* 37, no. 3 (May–June, 1959): 46–60.

Dofny, J., and David, Hélène. "Les aspirations des travailleurs de la métallurgie à Montréal." *Recherches Sociographiques* 6, no 1 (janvier–avril, 1965): 61–85.

Drucker, Peter F. "The Employee Society." *American Journal of Sociology* 58, no. 4 (January, 1953): 358–63.

Dubin, P. "Industrial Workers' Worlds: A Study of the Central Life Interests of Industrial Workers." *Social Problems* 3, no. 3 (January, 1955): 131–42.

Durand, C. "Conséquences de la modernisation sur l'évolution des relations de travail." *Journal de Psychologie Normale et Pathologique* 57, no. 2 (avril–juin, 1960): 177–92.

Foote, N. "The Professionalization of Labor in Detroit." *American Journal of Sociology* 58, no. 4 (January, 1953): 371–80.

Foote, N., and Hatt, Paul. "Social Mobility and Economic Advancement." *American Economics Association Papers and Proceedings* 65 (1953): 364–78.

Fortin, G., and Tremblay, Louis-Marie. "Attitudes à l'égard des occupations dans une paroisse agricole." *Recherches Sociographiques* 2, n° 1 (janvier–mars, 1961): 35–54.

Guest, R. H. "Work Careers and Aspirations of Mass Production Workers." *American Sociological Review* 19, no. 2 (April, 1954): 155–63.

Hecksher, A., and de Grazia, Sebastian. "Problems in Review: Executive Leisure." *Harvard Business Review* 37, no. 4 (July–August, 1959): 6 ff.

Inkeles, Alex. "Industrial Man: The Relation of Status to Experience, Perception and Values." *American Journal of Sociology* 66, no. 1 (July, 1960): 1–31.

Montague, J. T. "International Unions and the Canadian Trade Union Movement." *Canadian Journal of Economics and Political Science* 23, no. 1 (1957): 69–82.

Moos, Ida. "When the Computer Takes Over the Office." *Harvard Business Review* 38, no. 4 (1960): 102–12.

Nehnevajsu, J. "Automation and Social Stratification" in *Automation and Society*, edited by H. B. Jacobson and J. S. Roucek. New York: Philosophical Library, 1959.

Neufeld, E. P. "The Economic Significance of Consumer Credit in Canada," in *Consumer Credit in Canada*. University of Saskatchewan, Saskatoon Conference (1966): 5–19.

Reissman, Leonard. "Levels of Aspiration and Social Class." *American Sociological Review* 18, no. 3 (June, 1953): 233–42.

Tremblay, M. A. "Les tensions psychologiques chez le bucheron; quelques éléments d'explication." *Recherches Sociologiques* 1, n° 1 (janvier–mars, 1960): 61–82.

Ulman, Lloyd. "Influences of the Economic Environment on the Structure of the Steel Workers' Unions." *Proceedings of the Fourteenth Annual Meeting*. Industrial Relations Research Association. New York (December 28–29, 1961): 227–37.

Index

Alcan-Kingston experiment (Canada), 134

Alienation, 51–52, 83, 95, 112, 118, 123, 125, 126, 128, 129

Aspirations of workers, 59–60, 64, 92, 95–96, 116; for children, 90–91

Automation, 27, 43–48, 118; clerical workers' attitudes toward, 48; and equalitarianism, 49–50; and job hierarchies, 46–47, 50; and management, 47–48, 55–57; and office work, 53–54; and physical isolation, 46, 51, 57; production workers' attitudes toward, 48–49; and productivity, 93–94; and promotions, 94; and shift work, 93–94; skill and responsibility requirements of, 45–47, 57; skilled workers' attitudes toward, 48; and supervision, 47, 94; and unemployment, 45–47, 61; and wages, 47, 94; and white collar unionism, 54–55

Blue collar workers. See Workers, semiskilled, skilled, and unskilled. See also "Modern" worker and "Traditional" worker

Bulwarism, 116

Class consciousness, 16–17, 35–37, 39–41, 83–84, 98

Collective bargaining, 44, 107, 109–11, 117, 118

Consumers: investment expenditures, 6, 10; and credit or instalment buying, 11, 12–14; and discretionary income, 3, 7, 10–11, 12; and economic stability, 10–11

Consumption patterns: and age, 14–15, 17; and education, 10, 31; and income, 14, 16–17

Continuous process production. See Automation

Delinquents, 123

Demonstration effect, 19, 108–9

Distribution of rewards, 102, 105–6, 119, 121–22, 134

Downward mobility, 71

Economic development: and educational levels, 22–23; indices of, 3–4; "takeoff" period, 3, 6, 22

Education: and class voting, 39–41; and "financial option" return, 29–30; and individual income, 26–28; and industrial conflict, 41; and mobility, 28–31; and national economic growth, 25–26; and occupational class, 26–27; and occupational expectations, 31, 32–35, 41; and politi-